SHOPPING GUIDE FOR
CARING
CONSUMERS

A GUIDE TO PRODUCTS THAT ARE NOT TESTED ON ANIMALS

PEOPLE FOR THE ETHICAL TREATMENT OF ANIMALS

BOOK PUBLISHING COMPANY
SUMMERTOWN, TENNESSEE

PETA attempts to update this guide annually. However, we may not receive necessary information before going to print. Therefore, this guide is based on the most current information available at the time of printing. Companies not listed as cruelty-free may be cruelty-free but are not included because they have not sent PETA a letter stating their complete rejection of animal testing, nor signed PETA's Statement of Assurance. Companies identified as conducting animal tests may have changed their animal testing policies after this edition was printed. Inclusion on any list is not an endorsement of a company and/or any of its products by PETA. For periodically updated company information, please contact PETA.

PETA's updated 1998 *Shopping Guide for Caring Consumers* lists more than 550 cruelty-free cosmetics, household, and personal-care product companies, making it easy to find everything from hair color and furniture polish to correction fluid and more.

Cover photo of Lisa Rinna by T. C. Reiner

© 1997 PETA   ISBN 1-57067-048-X

The Book Publishing Company
P.O. Box 99
Summertown, TN 38483

Edited by Robyn Wesley
Proofread by Karen Porreca
Special thanks to Sandi Okun

PETA
People for the Ethical Treatment of Animals
501 Front St.
Norfolk, VA 23510
757-622-PETA

TABLE OF CONTENTS

FOREWORD

Dear Reader,

Helping animals is now easier than ever before. Every time you buy shampoo, toothpaste, soap, and other cosmetics and household products from a cruelty-free company, you are saying "no." to the painful and outdated product tests many companies still perform on animals. More than 550 companies, including industry giants like Revlon, Avon, and Estée Lauder, have signed PETA's Statement of Assurance guaranteeing that they do not test ingredients or finished products on animals—and the list continues to grow every day. Just this past year, The Gillette Company, whose animal testing PETA has campaigned against for more than a decade, declared that it is observing a moratorium (current suspension) on animal tests. Gillette's decision to stop animal tests was greatly influenced by the pressure of consumers who boycotted the company's products.

Sometimes products not tested on animals do cost a little more than other brands, but think of what you'll be saving: the lives of millions of animals who, without the actions of caring consumers like you, would still be subjected to Draize eye and skin irritancy tests and lethal dose tests. As consumer demand for cruelty-free products continues to grow, more and more companies are responding by using alternatives to animal tests such as tissue and cell cultures and computer models.

Many companies have also taken their commitment to helping animals a step further by using alternatives to animal ingredients. We encourage you to seek out vegan cosmetics and household products, and, to further assist you in living cruelty-free, we have added a new section to this year's guide which provides suggestions for finding vegan alternatives to leather and other animal products.

We have the power to speak out for those who cannot speak for themselves and demand an end to animal tests. By purchasing this book, you have taken the first step. The next step is to patronize the companies that are committed to producing safe, effective, and cruelty-free products—and to boycott those that aren't. With every cruelty-free purchase you make, you will experience the satisfaction of compassionate shopping, and you will be showing the world your respect for all life.

Thanks for caring!

THE SHOPPING GUIDE FOR CARING CONSUMERS

We are pleased to present the eighth edition of the *Shopping Guide for Caring Consumers*. The information in this booklet was compiled by People for the Ethical Treatment of Animals (PETA) as part of its international Cruelty-Free Product Campaign. PETA embarked

on this project to offer consumers a way to identify products manufactured by companies that do not test on animals.

The companies listed in this shopping guide have signed a Statement of Assurance or provided a company policy statement verifying that they:

1) do not conduct animal tests on ingredients or finished products;

2) do not contract with other laboratories to conduct animal tests; and

3) will not conduct animal tests in the future.

CORPORATE STANDARD OF COMPASSION FOR ANIMALS

PETA and eight other animal protection groups recently formed the Coalition for Consumer Information on Cosmetics to create a unified policy in order to make it easier for consumers and companies to identify the products that meet ethical standards. In addition to meeting PETA's three requirements listed above, the Corporate Standard of Compassion for Animals will require companies to obtain statements of assurance from all their suppliers to the effect that no animal tests were performed on ingredients supplied to them. We are currently collecting new data from companies, and the new standard should be reflected in the next edition of this guide.

ANIMAL TESTING FOR SAFETY: ABSOLUTELY UNNECESSARY

Every year, millions of animals suffer and die in painful tests allegedly to determine the safety of cosmetics, household, and other consumer products.

Two of the most notoriously cruel and unnecessary tests are the lethal dose tests and the Draize eye irritancy tests, which, while still in use today, date back to the 1920s. In the lethal dose tests, animals are force-fed, injected with, or forced to breathe the vapor of toxic substances until a designated percentage of the animals die. In the Draize eye tests, a substance is introduced into albino rabbits' eyes, usually without anesthesia. The rabbits are immobilized in stocks, their eyelids held open by clips. The rabbits are forced to endure these conditions for up to 18 days. Reactions include discharge, inflammation, ulceration, hemorrhage, and blindness.

Not only are these tests widely criticized in scientific circles because of their cruelty, results from these tests are unreliable and often contradictory. Federal regulatory agencies such as the Food and Drug Administration do not require the use of animals to test cosmetics and household products.

Thanks to modern technology, many companies have turned to non-animal tests. Human volunteers, *in vitro* methodology, computer models, cloned human skin, tissue cultures, and extensive databases are just a few of the sophisticated, reliable alternatives available.

LOOK FOR VEGAN INGREDIENTS

Many consumer products contain animal-derived ingredients. Slaughterhouse byproducts are often used in hair and skin care products and even in toothpastes and shaving creams. Many consumers choose not to buy products that contain these ingredients because their purchase subsidizes industries in which animal suffering is inherent.

Our definition of vegan includes ingredients that are plant- or mineral-derived or synthetic.

Aside from slaughterhouse byproducts, animal-derived ingredients include honey, beeswax, silk and silk byproducts, lanolin, and substances extracted from insects or sea creatures.

Many ingredients can be of either vegetable or animal origin. These ingredients include, but are not limited to, cetyl alcohol, glycerin, lecithin, mono- and diglycerides, stearic acid, and squalene. If in doubt about the origin of an ingredient, please check with the manufacturer.

Companies marked with a **V** in the guide manufacture all product lines without animal-derived ingredients. However, most of the companies listed in the guide make some vegan products even if their line is not strictly vegan. Please check with the companies for further information on these products.

CARING CONSUMER PRODUCT LOGO

Since 1990, PETA has made the Caring Consumer Product Logo available to cruelty-free companies. You can be sure that products displaying this certified trademark adhere to PETA's stringent standards.

WE HAVE BANNED ANIMAL TESTS & INGREDIENTS

Consumer Product Logo. Please look for information on the new logo in next year's guide, and, in the meantime, continue to look for PETA's Caring Consumer Product Logo on cruelty-free products.

For more information about product testing or other animal rights issues, please contact:

The Coalition for Consumer Information on Cosmetics (CCIC) will be introducing a product logo in conjunction with the Corporate Standard of Compassion for Animals. As part of the CCIC, PETA will be adopting this new logo in place of our existing Caring

People for the Ethical Treatment of Animals
501 Front St.
Norfolk, VA 23510
757-622-PETA

COMPANIES THAT DON'T TEST ON ANIMALS

What Types of Companies Are on the "Don't Test" list?

Some products are required by law to be tested on animals (e.g., pharmaceuticals, automotive and garden chemicals, food additives, etc.) Others are not (e.g., cosmetics, personal care, and household products). At the present time, PETA's Cruelty-Free Product Campaign is addressing only the issue of animal testing that is *not* required. Therefore, this list does not include companies that manufacture *only* products *required* to be tested on animals. What it does include are 1) companies that *only* manufacture products *not* required to be animal-tested and 2) companies that manufacture both products *required* to be animal-tested and products *not* required to be animal-tested. In order to be listed, however, each company has stated that it does *not* conduct any animal tests *not* required by law.

ABBA Products, Inc.
2010 Main St., #1000
Irvine, CA 92614
714-851-3955
800-848-4475
Products: aromatherapy, hair care, detoxifier, shampoo, conditioner, hair spray, permanents
Availability: fine hair salons, beauty supply stores
🖼 V

ABEnterprises
145 Cortlandt St.
Staten Island, NY
10302-2048
718-448-1526
Products: toiletries, household
Availability: mail order
MO

Abercrombie & Fitch
4 Limited Pkwy.
Reynoldsburg, OH
43068
614-577-6570
Products: fragrance for men, toiletries, personal care
Availability:
Abercrombie & Fitch stores, Victoria's Secret stores

Legend

🖼 Company using PETA's Caring Consumer product logo. (All companies listed in the guide are cruelty-free. Many of them have chosen to use our logo to assist consumers.)

V Vegan symbol. (Companies that manufacture strictly vegan products, i.e., containing no animal products. Companies without this symbol may offer some vegan products.)

MO Mail order available.

Abkit, Inc
207 E. 94th St.
Suite 201
New York, NY 10128
800-CAMOCARE
Products: skin care, hair
care, toiletries, household

Abracadabra, Inc.
10365 Hwy. 116
Forestville, CA 95436
707-869-0761
abrabath@aol.com
Products: toiletries
Availability: health food
stores, mail order
V MO

Adrien Arpel, Inc.
720 Fifth Ave., 8th Fl.
New York, NY 10019
212-333-7700
800-215-8333
Products: cosmetics, skin
care for men and women
Availability: department
stores

Advanage Wonder Cleaner
16615 S. Halsted St.
Harvey, IL 60426
708-333-7644
800-323-6444
Products: household, carpet/
rug cleaning supply,
furniture polish, oven
cleaner, automotive cleaner,
natural shaving lotion, hair
care, multipurpose cleaner,
aloe vera gel
Availability: Austin
Diversified stores, distributors, mail order
V MO

African Bio-Botanica, Inc.
602 NW Ninth Ave.
Gainesville, FL 32601
904-376-7329
Products: hair care, skin care
for men and women
Availability: beauty supply
stores, mail order
MO

Ahimsa Natural Care Ltd.
1250 Reid St., Suite 13A
Richmond Hill
Ontario L4B 1G3 Canada
905-709-8977
888-424-4672
AHIMSA@Interlog.com
Products: hair care, dandruff
shampoo, fragrance for men
and women, baby care,
aromatherapy
Availability: health food
stores, environmental stores,
cooperatives, boutiques/
specialty stores
≋ V MO

Alba Naturals
P.O. Box 40339
Santa Barbara, CA 93140
805-965-0170
800-347-5211
Products: baby care, skin
care, sun care, toiletries,
bathing supply, soap,
shaving supply
Availability: drugstores,
health food stores, cooperatives, boutiques, specialty
stores, mail order
MO

**Alexandra Avery Body
Botanicals**
4717 S.E. Belmont
Portland, OR 97215
503-236-5926
800-669-1863
Products: aromatherapy,
baby care, condoms/
lubricants, fragrance, hypo-
allergenic skin care, sun
care, toiletries, bathing
supply, soap, shaving supply
Availability: mail order,
health food stores, cooperatives, boutiques, specialty
stores, salons
MO

**Alexandra de Markoff
(Parlux)**
3725 S.W. 30th Ave.
Ft. Lauderdale, FL 33312
954-316-9008
800-727-5895
Products: cosmetics
Availability: department
stores

Allens Naturally
P.O. Box 514, Dept. M
Farmington, MI 48332-0514
313-453-5410
800-352-8971
Products: household,
laundry detergent
Availability: health food
stores, cooperatives,
supermarkets, mail order
≋ V MO

9

OUR CUSTOMERS ARE PRETTY SMART

Our customers want affordable, high quality, vegan products without petrochemicals, sodium lauryl & laureth sulfates, cocomide DEA, artificial fragrances, artificial colors unnecessary fillers, thickeners, parabens, animal products & mineral oils. We wouldn't want anything less for ourselves.

by Ahimsa

We offer a full line of Personal care products including hair care, skin care, massage oils, aromatherapy baths & shower gels, dandruff shampoos, full baby products line and much more. All our products display the PETA caring consumer logo.

We're sure you fit this description. If you are not using our products yet it's probably because we have not entered the U.S. marketplace. Until we do you can order our products by calling us for a catalogue or to place an order. We will ship your order anywhere in the U.S. & Canada. See coupon in back for our eighth anniversary half price offer.

Ahimsa Natural Beauty,
1250 Reid St. #13A
Richmond Hill, Ontario Canada
L4B 1G3
tel (905)709-8977 fax (905) 709-0563
Distributor & retailer inquiries invited.

Almay (Revlon)
625 Madison Ave.
New York, NY 10022
212-572-5000
Products: cosmetics, deodorant, hypo-allergenic skin care for men and women, sun care
Availability: drugstores, grocery stores, department stores

Aloegen Natural Cosmetics
9200 Mason Ave.
Chatsworth, CA 91311
818-882-2951
800-327-2012
Products: skin care
Availability: health food stores, cooperatives, mail order
MO

Aloette Cosmetics, Inc.
1301 Wright's La. E.
West Chester, PA 19380
610-692-0600
800-ALOETTE
102503.3221@compuserve.com
Products: cosmetics, sun care, fragrance for men and women, skin care for men and women, nail care, toiletries, hair care
Availability: Aloette franchises

Aloe Up, Inc.
P.O. Box 831
6908 W. Expressway 83
Harlingen, TX 78551
210-428-0081
800-537-2563
Products: hair care, hypo-allergenic skin care for men and women, sun care, toiletries
Availability: health food stores, supermarkets, drugstores, boutiques, specialty stores, mail order
MO

Aloe Vera of America, Inc.
9660 Dilworth Rd.
Dallas, TX 75243
214-343-5700
Products: toiletries, skin care
Availability: distributors

Alvin Last, Inc.
19 Babcock Place
Yonkers, NY 10701
914-376-1000
800-527-8123
Products: hair care, dandruff shampoo, hair color (henna), dental hygiene, toiletries, shaving supply, cosmetics, skin care for men and women
Availability: health food stores, drugstores, mail order
MO

10

Amazon Premium Products
P.O. Box 530156
Miami, FL 33153
305-757-1943
800-832-5645
enviroworld@worldnet.att.net
http://www.amazonpp.com
Products: Enviro-Magic
brand, household, furniture
polish, boat-cleaning supply,
stainless steel cleaning
supply for home, auto, and
industrial use, teak wood
cleaning supply
Availability: health food
stores, hardware stores,
marine stores, boutiques,
mail order
V MO

**American Formulating &
Manufacturing**
350 W. Ash St., Suite 700
San Diego, CA 92101
619-239-0321
Products: paint, stain,
cleaners, adhesive,
household, carpet/rug
cleaning supply, hair care
Availability: distributors,
health food stores, "green"
stores, building contractors,
mail order
V MO

American International
2220 Gaspar Ave.
Los Angeles, CA 90040
213-728-2999
Products: skin care, toiletries
Availability: discount
department stores, supermarkets, drugstores, boutiques,
specialty stores, beauty
supply, health food stores

**American Safety Razor
Company**
P.O. Box 500
Staunton, VA 24402
540-248-8000
800-445-9284
Products: aromatherapy,
toiletries, bathing, soap,
razors, blades, shaving
supply (Personna, Flicker,
Burma Shave, Gem, Bump
Fighter)
Availability: PETA catalog,
department stores, discount
department stores, drug-
stores, health food stores,
supermarkets, boutiques,
specialty stores, mail order
🖼 MO

**America's Finest Products
Corporation**
1639 Ninth St.
Santa Monica, CA 90404
310-450-6555
800-482-6555
Products: household laundry
and cleaning, laundry soil-
stain remover, cool water
wash for delicates, multipurpose cleaner, concrete
cleaner, elbow grease, liquid
cleaner, water softener
Availability: supermarkets,
drugstores, mail order
V MO

Amitée Cosmetics
(Advanced Research Labs)
151 Kalmus Dr., Suite H3
Costa Mesa, CA 92626
714-556-1028
800-966-6960
aduva@advancedresearch.com
Products: hair care
Availability: supermarkets,
drugstores, beauty supply
stores

Amoresse Laboratories
4121 Buchanan St.
Riverside, CA 92503
800-258-7931
Products: nail care
Availability: salons

Amway Corporation
7575 E. Fulton Rd.
Ada, MI 49355-0001
616-787-6279
www.amway.com
Products: baby care, animal
care, cosmetics, dental,
feminine, fragrance, hair
care, dandruff, air freshener,
household, bleach, carpet
cleaning supply, laundry,
sun care, vitamin, car care,
furniture polish
Availability: distributors,
mail order
MO

Ananda Collection
14618 Tyler Foote Rd.
Nevada City, CA 95959
916-478-7575
800-537-8766
tacjoy@nccn.net
Products: fragrance for men
and women, household, air
freshener, massage oil
Availability: drugstores,
health food stores, co-ops,
boutiques, specialty stores,
mail order
V MO

Ancient Formulas, Inc.
638 W. 33rd St. N.
Wichita, KS 67204
800-543-3026
ancient@feist.com
Products: hypo-allergenic/
acne skin care for men and
women, herbal supplements
for blood pressure and
respiratory health, sleeping
aid, carbohydrate balance,
irregularity, prostate health
Availability: health food
stores, mail order, doctors
MO

**Andrea International
Industries**
2220 Gaspar Ave.
Los Angeles, CA 90040
213-728-2999
Products: nail care, skin care
for women
Availability: supermarkets,
drugstores, mass retailers,
discount department stores,
boutiques, specialty stores

Aramis, Inc. (Estée Lauder)
767 Fifth Ave.
New York, NY 10153
212-572-3700
Products: fragrance for men
and women, hair care,
razors, skin care for men,
sun care, toiletries, bathing
supply, deodorant, soap,
shaving cream/lotion
Availability: department
stores, specialty stores

Arbonne International, Inc.
P.O. Box 2488
Laguna Hills, CA 92654
800-ARBONNE
www.arbonneinternational.com
Products: cosmetics, skin
care
Availability: distributors
MO

Ardell International, Inc.
2220 Gaspar Ave.
Los Angeles, CA 90040
213-728-2999
Products: nail care, skin care
for women
Availability: supermarkets,
drugstores, mass retailers,
boutiques, specialty stores,
discount department stores

**Arizona Natural Resources,
Inc.**
2525 E. Beardsley Rd.
Phoenix, AZ 85024
602-569-6900
Products: cosmetics, sun
care, hair care, toiletries,
baby care, hypo-allergenic
skin care for men and
women
Availability: distributors,
discount department stores,
drugstores, health food
stores, supermarkets,
boutiques, warehouse clubs
MO

Aromaland, Inc.
1326 Rufina Cir.
Santa Fe, NM 87505
505-438-0402
800-933-5267
www.aromaland.com
Products: fragrance for men
and women, essential oil-
diffusing lamps, car air
freshener, aromatherapy
books, essential oil
Availability: health food
stores, cooperatives,
department stores, salons,
drugstores, boutiques,
specialty stores, spas, mail
order
V MO

Aroma Vera, Inc.
5901 Rodeo Rd.
Los Angeles, CA 90016-
4312
310-280-0407
800-669-9514
www.aromavera.com
Products: aromatherapy,
fragrance for men and
women, hair care, air
freshener, skin care for men
and women, toiletries,
bathing supply, soap, gift
items
Availability: health food
stores, Aroma Vera stores,
boutiques, specialty stores,
salons, spas, mail order
MO

Astonish Industries Inc.
Commerce Lane Business
Park
423 Commerce La., Unit 2
Berlin, NJ 08091
609-753-7078
609-753-8421
Products: household
cleaning supply, air
freshener, dishwashing
liquid, antibacterial cleanser,
sponges, cleaning cloths,
nonscratch scouring pads,
travel supply
Availability: drugstores,
health food stores, supermarkets, specialty stores, mail
order
V MO

**Atmosa Brand
Aromatherapy Products**
1420 Fifth Ave., 22nd Fl.
Suite 2200
Seattle, WA 98101-2378
206-521-5986
206-621-6567
Products: aromatherapy and
home fragrance
Availability: boutiques,
department stores, specialty
stores
V

Aubrey Organics, Inc.
4419 N. Manhattan Ave.
Tampa, FL 33614
813-877-4186
800-AUBREYH
http://www.aubrey-organics.com
Products: cosmetics, toiletries, hair care, baby care, companion animal care, fragrance for men and women, household, hypo-allergenic skin care, sun care, shaving supply, deodorant
Availability: health food stores, mail order
MO

Aunt Bee's Skin Care
P.O. Box 2678
Rancho de Taos, NM 87577
505-737-0522
Products: lip balm, skin care, personal care
Availability: health food stores, mail order, drug-stores, supermarkets
MO

Aura Cacia, Inc.
P.O. 311
Norway, IN 52318
800-437-3301
info@frontierherb.com
Products: aromatherapy, baby care, fragrances for men and women, skin care, toiletries, bathing supply, soap
Availability: discount department stores, drug-stores, health food stores, cooperatives, boutiques, specialty stores
V MO

Auroma International
P.O. Box 1008
Silver Lake, WI 53170
414-889-8501
Products: fragrance for men and women, household, air freshener, dental hygiene, toiletries, incense
Availability: drugstores, health food stores, supermar-kets, cooperatives, mail order
V MO

Legend
🏠 Company uses Caring Consumer product logo
V Vegan symbol (products contain no animal ingredients)
MO Mail order available

Auromère Ayurvedic Imports
2621 W. Highway 12
Lodi, CA 95242
209-339-3710
800-735-4691
Products: toiletries, dental hygiene, skin care for men and women, ayurvedic, incense, massage oil
Availability: health food stores, cooperatives, boutiques, specialty stores, New Age, environmental stores, mail order

Australasian College of Herbal Studies
P.O. Box 57
Lake Oswego, OR 97034
503-635-6652
800-487-8839
achs@herbed.com
Products: aromatherapy
Availability: mail order

Autumn-Harp, Inc.
61 Pine St.
Bristol, VT 04551
802-453-4807
Products: baby care, sun care, cosmetics, aromatherapy, nonperscription therapy, personal care
Availability: health food stores, cooperatives, drugstores, grocery stores, mail order, department stores

Aveda Corporation
4000 Pheasant Ridge Dr.
Blaine, MN 55449
612-783-4000
800-328-0849
www.aveda.com
Products: cosmetics, hair care, skin care, "pure-fume" (R), lifestyle items
Availability: fine salons, spas, environmental lifestyle stores, health care facilities, educational institutions

Avigal Henna
45-49 Davis St.
Long Island City, NY 11101
800-722-1011
Products: henna hair color
Availability: health food stores, salons, specialty stores

Avon
9 W. 57th St.
New York, NY 10019
212-546-6015
800-858-8000
http:www.avon.com
Products: cosmetics, fragrance for men and women, hair care, dandruff shampoo, hypo-allergenic skin care for men and women, nail care, toiletries, sun care, Skin So Soft insect repellant
Availability: distributors

Ayurherbal Corporation
1100 Lotus Dr.
Silver Lake, WI 53170
414-889-8569
Products: fragrance for men and women, household, air freshener, dental hygiene, toiletries, incense
Availability: health food stores, drugstores, cooperatives, boutiques, specialty stores, mail order
V **MO**

Ayurveda Holistic Center
82A Bayville Ave.
Bayville, NY 11709
516-628-8200
mail@ayurveda.com
Products: ayurvedic herbs for humans and companion animals
Availability: health food stores, ayurveda holistic center stores, cooperatives, boutiques, specialty stores, yoga centers
V

Ayus/Oshadhi
15 Monarch Bay Plaza
Suite 346
Monarch Beach, CA 92629
714-240-1104
800-933-1008
Products: fragrance for men and women, aromatherapy oil, hair oil, air freshener, skin care for men and women, aromatherapy diffusers, essential oil, massage oil
Availability: health food stores, distributors, health spas, boutiques, specialty stores, aromatherapists
 V **MO**

Barbizon International, Inc.
1900 Glades Rd., Suite 300
Boca Raton, FL 33431
407-362-8883
Products: cosmetics, skin care for men and women, nail care
Availability: Barbizon schools, mail order
 MO

Bare Escentuals
600 Townsend St., Suite 329-E
San Francisco, CA 94103
415-487-3400
800-227-3990
Products: cosmetics, fragrance for men and women, hair care, shaving supply, hypo-allergenic skin care for men and women, nail care, sun care, toiletries, aromatherapy, massage oil
Availability: department stores, Bare Escentuals stores
V

Basic Elements Hair Care System, Inc.
505 S. Beverly Dr.
Suite 1292
Beverly Hills, CA 90212
800-947-5522
Products: hair care, skin care for men and women
Availability: salons, mail order
 MO

Legend

    Company uses Caring Consumer product logo

V Vegan symbol (products contain no animal ingredients)

MO Mail order available

Basically Natural
109 E. G St.
Brunswick, MD 21716
301-834-7923
Products: baby care, companion animal care, cosmetics, dental hygiene, hair care, household, air freshener, bleach, detergent, oven cleaner, hypo-allergenic skin care for men and women, sun care, toiletries, deodorant, shaving supply
Availability: mail order nationally; local customers may choose from stock, by appointment
V **MO**

Bath and Body Works
97 W. Main St.
New Albany, OH 43054
800-395-1001
Products: hair care, dandruff shampoo, fragrance for men and women, skin care for men and women, sun care, toiletries, shaving supply
Availability: Express stores, Bath and Body Works stores

Bath Island, Inc.
469 Amsterdam Ave.
New York, NY 10024
212-787-9415
Products: aromatherapy, baby care, dental hygiene, toothbrushes, fragrance, hair care, dandruff shampoo, household, air freshener, nail care, skin care, sun care, toiletries, deodorant, soap, shaving supply, vitamins
Availability: Bath Island stores, mail order
MO

BECAUSE YOU RESPECT LIFE

Basically Natural

**No animal testing - No animal-derived ingredients
environmentally sound**
Personal Care . . Cosmetics . . Household . . Companion Animal
FREE MAIL ORDER CATALOG

**109 East G Street
Brunswick, MD 21716
(301) 834-7923   1-800-352-7099**

Baudelaire, Inc.
166 Emerald St.
Keene, NH 03431
603-352-9234
800-327-2324
Products: baby care, dental
hygiene, hair care, toiletries,
soap, aromatherapy,
personal care
Availability: department
stores, health food stores,
boutiques, specialty stores,
mail order
MO

BeautiControl Cosmetics
2121 Midway Rd.
Carrollton, TX 75006
972-458-0601
Products: skin care,
cosmetics, fragrance for
men, fragrance for women,
nail care, sun care, hypo-
allergenic skin care
Availability: distributors

Beauty Naturally, Inc
P.O. Box 4905
859 Cowan Rd.
Burlingame, CA 94011-4905
415-697-7547
800-432-4323
info@beautynaturally.com
Products: hair care, skin
care, toiletries, hair color,
permanents
Availability: health food
stores, mail order
MO

Beauty Without Cruelty
Cosmetics
P.O. Box 750428
Petaluma, CA 94975-0428
707-769-5120
Products: aromatherapy,
cosmetics, hair care, hypo-
allergenic skin care for
men and women, sun care,
bathing supply, toiletries
Availability: department
stores, health food stores,
beauty supply stores,
boutiques, specialty stores,
salons, mail order
MO

Beehive Botanicals, Inc.
Rte. 8, Box 8257
Hayward, WI 54843
715-634-4274
800-233-4483
beehive@win.bright.net
Products: hair care, dental
hygiene, hypo-allergenic
skin care for men and
women, toiletries
Availability: health food
stores, cooperatives,
drugstores, mail order
MO

Beiersdorf, Inc.
BDF Plaza
360 Martin Luther King Dr.
Norwalk, CT 06856-5529
203-853-8008
Products: skin care for men
and women, Nivea, Eucerin,
Basis soap, La Prairie
Availability: grocery stores,
drugstores

17

Bella's Secret Garden
1601 Emerson Ave.
Channel Islands, CA 93463
805-483-5750
800-962-6867
Products: toiletries, fragrance for women, baby care, hair care, household, air freshener, hypo-allergenic skin care for men and women
Availability: department stores, drugstores, boutiques, small gift stores

Belle Star, Inc.
23151 Alcalde, #A-1
Laguna Hills, CA 92653
714-768-7006
800-442-STAR
mickeylynne@msn.com
Products: fragrance for men and women, toiletries, incense, aromatherapy supply
Availability: Belle Star store, craft shows, boutiques, specialty stores, mail order
▨ MO

Berol (Sanford Corp.)
2711 Washington Blvd.
Bellwood, IL 60104
708-547-5525
800-438-3703
Products: office supply
Availability: office supply stores, drugstores, grocery stores
MO

Better Botanicals
3066 M St. N.W.
Washington, DC 20007
202-625-6815
888-BB-HERBS
bbherbs@betterbotanicals.com
www.betterbotanicals.com
Products: aromatherapy, hair care, skin care, toiletries
Availability: Better Botanicals stores, mail order, health food stores
MO

Beverly Hills Cold Wax
P.O. Box 600476
San Diego, CA 92160
619-283-0880
800-833-0889
Products: cold wax, toiletries
Availability: health food stores, mail order
MO

Beverly Hills Cosmetic Group
289 S. Robertson Blvd., #461
Beverly Hills, CA 90211
800-277-1069
Products: cosmetics, fragrance
Availability: department stores, boutiques

BioFilm, Inc.
3121 Scott St.
Vista, CA 92083
619-727-9030
800-848-5900
lisaoc@biofilm.com
Products: Astroglide personal lubricant
Availability: drugstores
V

Biogime
1665 Townhurst, #100
Houston, TX 77043
713-827-1972
800-338-8784
Products: hypo-allergenic skin care for men and women, sun care, toiletries, nutrition supply
Availability: distributors, Biogime stores
V MO

Biokosma
121 Fieldcrest Ave.
Edison, NJ 08818
201-225-2181
800-326-0500
Products: toiletries
Availability: specialty stores, mail order
MO

Bio-Tec Cosmetics, Inc.
92 Sherwood Ave.
Toronto, Ontario M4P 2A7
Canada
800-667-2524
Products: hair care, permanents, hair coloring, skin care for men and women, toiletries, cosmetics
Availability: hair care in beauty salons, bath and skin care in retail outlets

Biotone
4564 Alvarado Canyon Rd., #1
San Diego, CA 92120
619-281-4228
Products: massage cream and oil for therapists, hypo-allergenic
Availability: distributors, direct to massage therapists

Black Pearl Gardens
220 Maple St.
Franklin, OH 45005
513-743-8761
800-891-0142
Products: toiletries, fragrance for women, baby care
Availability: mail order, specialty stores
MO

Bobbi Brown
767 Fifth Ave.
New York, NY 10153
212-572-4200
Products: cosmetics
Availability: department stores

Bo-Chem Company, Inc.
(Neway)
42 Doaks La.
Marblehead, MA 01945
617-631-9400
Products: household
Availability: distributors
MO

Body Encounters
604 Manor Rd.
Cinnamonson, NJ 08077
609-829-4660
800-839-2639
Products: aromatherapy, hair
care, skin care, sun care,
toiletries, bathing supply,
soap, shaving cream/lotion
Availability: mail order
MO

Bodyography
1641 16th St.
Santa Monica, CA 90404
310-399-2886
800-642-2639
Products: baby care, hair
care, dandruff shampoo,
hypo-allergenic skin care
for men and women,
toiletries, cosmetics, shaving
supply, fragrance for men
and women
Availability: Bodyography
stores, department stores,
select duty-free shops

Body Shop, Inc.
P.O. Box 1409
Wake Forest, NC 27588
800-541-2535
http://www.the-body-shop.com
Products: aromatherapy,
baby care, cosmetics, dental
hygiene, toothbrushes,
fragrance, hair care, hair
color, nail care, razors, skin
care, sun care, toiletries,
bathing supply, deodorant,
soap, shaving supply
Availability: Body Shop
stores, mail order
MO

Body Suite
515 N. Broad St.
San Luis Obispo, CA 93405
805-781-5754
bodysuite@6.net
www.bodysuite.com
Products: baby care,
companion animal care,
cosmetics, hair care, sun
care, fragrance for men and
women, dandruff shampoo,
air fresheners, permanents,
household, hypo-allergenic
skin care
Availability: Body Suite
stores, distributors
⚱ V MO

Body Time
1341 Seventh St.
Berkeley, CA 94710
415-524-0360
Products: toiletries,
fragrance for men and
women, hair care, skin care,
sun care, air freshener,
aromatherapy, shaving
supply, essential oils,
massage oil and lotion
Availability: Body Time
stores

Bon Ami/Faultless Starch
510 Walnut St.
Kansas City, MO 64106-
1209
816-842-1230
Products: household
cleaning supply
Availability: grocery stores,
drugstores

Bonne Bell
18519 Detroit Ave.
Georgetown Row
Lakewood, OH 44107
216-221-0800
Products: cosmetics, sun
care, skin care, bathing
supply
Availability: drugstores,
supermarkets, department
stores, discount department
stores

Börlind of Germany
P.O. Box 130
New London, NH 03257
603-526-2076
800-447-7024
Products: cosmetics, hair
care, toiletries,
aromatherapy
Availability: health food
stores, boutiques, specialty
stores, salons, spas

Botan Corporation
3708 W. Broadway, Suite 1
Louisville, KY 40211
502-772-0800
800-448-0800
Products: hypo-allergenic
skin care for men and
women, toiletries, shaving
lotion
Availability: health food
stores, department stores,
distributors, fine pharmacies,
specialty stores, green
boutique bath stores
V MO

Botanicus Retail, Inc.
7610 T. Rickenbacker Dr.
Gaithersburg, MD 20879
301-977-8887
800-282-8887
Products: toiletries, fragrance for men and women, household, air freshener, hypo-allergenic skin care for men and women
Availability: department stores, drugstores, health food stores, Botanicus Retail stores, boutiques, mail order
MO

Brocato International
1 Main St., Suite 501
Woodburg, MN 55414
800-243-0275
Products: hair care, permanents
Availability: salons, barber shops
V

Bronson Pharmaceuticals
1945 Craig Rd.
St. Louis, MO 63146
800-521-3322
Products: cosmetics, vitamins, minerals, food supplements
Availability: drugstores, health food stores, mail order
MO

Bronzo Sensualé
945 41st St., Suite 202
Miami, FL 33140
305-531-2992
800-991-2226
Products: sun care, aromatherapy, skin care
V MO

Brookside Soap Company
P.O. Box 55638
Seattle, WA 98155
206-742-2265
Products: soap, companion animal care
Availability: health food stores, grocery stores in Washington, mail order
V MO

Caeran, Inc.
210 King George Rd.
Brantford, Ontario N3R 5Y5
Canada
519-751-0513
800-563-2974
Products: carpet/rug cleaning supply, cosmetics, hair care, laundry detergent, household, vitamins, car care, nonprescription therapy, personal care
Availability: mail order, health food stores
MO

California Skin Therapy
1100 Glendon Ave.
Suite 1250
Los Angeles, CA 90024
213-824-4041
800-927-7873
Products: skin care for men and women, self-tanning products
Availability: salons

CamoCare Camomile Skin Care Products
207 E. 94th St.
Suite 201
New York, NY 10128
212-860-8358
800-CAMOCARE
Products: natural skin care based on camomile, facial care, body care, hair care, feminine hygiene supply, toiletries
Availability: health food stores, cooperatives, nutrition sections in mass market stores

Candy Kisses Natural Lip Balm
16 E. 40th St., 12th Fl.
New York, NY 10016
212-951-3035
candykiss@beautycology.com
Products: cosmetics
Availability: mail order, discount department stores, drugstores, supermarkets
V MO

Carina Supply, Inc.
464 Granville St.
Vancouver, British Columbia
V6C 1V4
Canada
604-687-3617
Products: hair care, dandruff shampoo, hair color, permanents, hypo-allergenic skin care for men and women, companion animal care
Availability: Carina Supply stores, salons, companion animal supply stores, groomers, veterinarians, mail order
MO

Caring Catalog
7678 Sagewood Dr.
Huntington Beach, CA 92648
714-842-0454
Products: aromatherapy, baby care, animal care, cosmetics, dental, toothbrushes, fragrance, dandruff shampoo, air freshener, household, bleach, carpet cleaner, laundry, nail care, skin care, sun care, toiletries, deodorant
Availability: mail order
MO

Carlson Laboratories, Inc.
15 College Dr.
Arlington Heights, IL 60004
847-255-1600
800-323-4141
Products: hair care, skin care, toiletries, vitamin supplements, natural personal care
Availability: health food stores

Carma Laboratories, Inc.
5801 W. Airways Ave.
Franklin, WI 53132
414-421-7707
Products: Carmex lip balm/cold sore medicine, nonperscription therapy, personal care
Availability: supermarkets, drugstores, mail order, health food stores, cooperatives
MO

Caswell-Massey
121 Fieldcrest Ave.
Edison, NJ 08818
201-225-2181
800-326-0500
Products: aromatherapy, baby care, dental, toothbrushes, fragrance, hair care, air freshener, razors, skin care, toiletries, bathing supply, deodorant, soap, shaving supply
Availability: department stores, Caswell-Massey stores, boutiques, specialty stores, mail order
MO

Celestial Body
21298 Pleasant Hill Rd.
Boonville, MO 65233
816-882-6858
Products: aromatherapy, hair care, fragrance for men and women, shaving supply, skin care, cosmetics, toiletries
Availability: health food stores, mail order
MO

Chanel, Inc.
9 W. 57th St.
New York, NY 10019
212-688-5055
Products: fragrance for men and women, cosmetics, skin care for men and women, nail care, sun care, toiletries, shaving supply
Availability: department stores, boutiques, specialty stores, beauty supply stores

Chatoyant Pearl Cosmetics
P.O. Box 526
Port Townsend, WA 98368
206-385-4825
Products: skin care, toiletries
Availability: health food stores

Chica Bella, Inc.
Interlink 580
P.O. Box 02-5635
Miami, FL 33152
408-457-4223
Products: hair care, baby care, skin care, toiletries, sun care, shaving supply
Availability: health food stores, supermarkets, cooperatives

CHIP Distribution Company
8321 Croydon Ave.
Los Angeles, CA 90045
310-545-8933
800-560-6753
Products: household, industrial/commercial supply
Availability: distributors, mail order
V MO

Christian Dior Perfumes, Inc.
9 W. 57th St.
New York, NY 10019
212-759-1840
Products: cosmetics, fragrance for men and women, skin care for men and women, skin care, nail care, toiletries
Availability: department stores, boutiques, specialty stores

Christine Valmy, Inc.
285 Change Bridge Rd.
Pine Brook, NJ 07058
201-575-1050
800-526-5057
Products: cosmetics, hypoallergenic skin care for men and women, sun care, shaving supply, toiletries
Availability: salons, J.C. Penney stores, spas, mail order
MO

Chuckles, Inc.
P.O. Box 5126
Manchester, NH 03109
603-669-4228
800-221-3496
Products: hair care, hair color, permanents
Availability: salons

CiCi Cosmetics
9500 W. Jefferson Blvd.
Culver City, CA 90232
213-272-3657
800-869-1224
Products: cosmetics
Availability: discount
department stores, drug-
stores, boutiques, specialty
stores, mail order, beauty
and theatrical supply stores
MO

Cinema Secrets, Inc.
4400 Riverside Dr.
Burbank, CA 91505
818-846-0579
Products: cosmetics,
theatrical makeup
Availability: beauty supply
stores, salons, costume/
novelty stores, Cinema
Secrets stores, mail order
V MO

Citius USA, Inc.
120 Interstate North Pkwy. E.
Suite 106
Atlanta, GA 30339
770-953-3663
800-343-9099
Products: environmentally
safe correction fluid, office
supply
Availability: office supply
stores, independent sales
representatives, Sanford
Corporation
 V

**Citré Shine (Advanced
Research Labs)**
151 Kalmus Dr., Suite H3
Costa Mesa, CA 92626
714-556-1028
800-966-6960
Products: hair care
Availability: supermarkets,
drugstores, beauty supply
stores

Clarins of Paris
135 E. 57th St.
New York, NY 10022
212-980-1800
Products: cosmetics, hypo-
allergenic skin care, sun
care, nail care, fragrance for
women, toiletries
Availability: department
stores, boutiques, specialty
stores

**Clearly Natural Products,
Inc.**
1340 N. McDowell Blvd.
Petaluma, CA 94954
707-762-5815
cnatu31924@aol.com
Products: vegetable glycerin
soaps, liquid glycerin soap
Availability: health food
stores, drugstores, supermarkets

Clear Vue Products, Inc.
P.O. Box 567
417 Canal St.
Lawrence, MA 01842
508-683-7151
508-794-3100
Products: window cleaner,
household
Availability: grocery stores in
New England, mail order
V MO

Clientele, Inc.
14101 N.W. Fourth St.
Sunrise, FL 33325
954-845-9500
800-327-4660
Products: cosmetics,
fragrance for men and
women, hair care, hypo-
allergenic skin care for men
and women, sun care,
theatrical makeup, toiletries,
vitamins
Availability: department
stores, boutiques, specialty
stores, mail order
MO

Clinique Laboratories, Inc.
767 Fifth Ave.
New York, NY 10153
212-572-3800
Products: cosmetics,
fragrance, hair care, nail
care, allergy-tested skin care,
sun care, toiletries, bathing
supply, deodorant, soap,
shaving supply
Availability: department
stores, specialty stores

Colorations, Inc.
2875 Berkeley Lake Rd.
Duluth, GA 30096
770-417-1501
Products: art and school
supply for children
Availability: school supply,
toy, and gift stores
V

Color Me Beautiful
14000 Thunderbolt Place
Suite E
Chantilly, VA 22021
703-471-6400
800-533-5503
Products: cosmetics, skin
care for men and women,
sun care, shaving supply
Availability: department
stores, drugstores, boutiques,
specialty stores, independent
sales representatives, mail
order
MO

Color My Image, Inc.
5025B Backlick Rd.
Annandale, VA 22003
703-354-9797
Products: cosmetics, nail
care, hypo-allergenic skin
care, sun care, theatrical
makeup, toiletries, bathing
supply, camouflage makeup
Availability: Color My Image
stores, mail order
MO

Columbia Cosmetics Manufacturing, Inc.
1661 Timothy Dr.
San Leandro, CA 94577
510-562-5900
800-824-3328
Products: cosmetics, fragrance for men and women, hair care, skin care, theatrical makeup, nail care
Availability: boutiques, specialty stores, distributors, mail order

Comfort Manufacturing Co.
1056 W. Van Buren St.
Chicago, IL 60607
312-421-8145
Products: dental hygiene, shaving supply, skin care
Availability: beauty supply stores, department stores, drugstores, supermarkets, mail order

Common Scents
128 Main St.
Port Jefferson, NY 11777
516-473-6370
Products: aromatherapy, baby care, toothbrushes, dental hygiene, fragrance, household, air freshener, skin care for women, toiletries, bathing supply, deodorant, soap, shaving supply
Availability: Common Scents stores, mail order

Compar, Inc.
70 E. 55th St.
New York, NY 10022
212-980-9620
Products: toiletries, fragrance for men and women
Availability: department stores

Compassionate Consumer
P.O. Box 27
Jericho, NY 11753
718-359-3983
800-733-4134
Products: cosmetics, toiletries, household, leather substitutes
Availability: mail order

Compassionate Cosmetics
P.O. Box 3534
Glendale, CA 91201
Products: cosmetics, toiletries, perfumes
Availability: mail order

Compassion Matters
2 E. Fourth St.
Jamestown, NY 14701
716-664-7023
Products: aromatherapy, baby care, animal care, cosmetics, dental, toothbrushes, fragrance, hair care, hair color, household, air freshener, bleach, laundry, razors, skin care, sun care, toiletries, vitamins
Availability: Compassion Matters store, mail order

Conair Corp.
1 Cummings Point Rd.
Stamford, CT 06904
203-351-9000
800-7-CONAIR
Products: Jheri Redding, hair care, permanents, toiletries, Conair haircare styling tools
Availability: drugstores, supermarkets, discount department stores, beauty supply stores

Concept Now Cosmetics (CNC)
P.O. Box 3208
Santa Fe Springs, CA 90670
310-903-1450
800-CNC-1215
Products: cosmetics, skin care for men and women, sun care
Availability: distributors, mail order

Cosmair (L'Oréal)
575 Fifth Ave.
New York, NY 10017
212-818-1500
Products: cosmetics, fragrance for men and women, hair color, nail care
Availability: department stores, drugstores, supermarkets, boutiques, specialty stores
Note: Cosmair does not test its products on animals. It may, however, test its ingredients on animals.

Cosmyl, Inc.
1 Cosmyl Pl.
Columbus, GA 31907
706-569-6100
800-262-4401
Products: cosmetics, fragrance for women, skin care for men and women, toiletries, nail care
Availability: J.C. Penney stores, Sears stores, department stores, boutiques, specialty stores

Cot 'n Wash, Inc.
502 The Times Bldg.
Ardmore, PA 19003
610-896-4373
800-355-WASH
Products: household, soap
for fine washables
Availability: health food
stores, cooperatives,
boutiques/specialty stores,
department stores, mail
order

Country Comfort
28537 Nuevo Valley Dr.
Nuevo, CA 92567
909-928-4038
800-462-6617
Products: baby care, healing
salve, lip balm
Availability: health food
stores, cooperatives, mail
order
 MO

Country Save Corporation
3410 Smith Ave.
Everett, WA 98201
206-258-1171
Products: household,
chlorine-free bleach,
laundry detergent, automatic
dishwashing powder
Availability: health food
stores, supermarkets,
cooperatives, available in
Canada at select stores
V

Countryside Fragrances
Pacific First Centre, 22nd Fl.
1420 Fifth Ave.
Seattle, WA 98101-2378
206-386-5886
800-447-8901
Products: potpourri,
wardrobe sachets, essential
oil, aromatherapy oil,
simmering potpourri,
mulling spices for cider and
wine
Availability: wholesale to
other companies, depart-
ment stores, boutiques

Crabtree & Evelyn Ltd.
Peake Brook Rd.
Box 167
Woodstock, CT 06281
203-928-2761
800-624-5211
Products: baby care,
fragrance for men and
women, razors, air freshener,
toothbrushes, toiletries,
shaving supply
Availability: Crabtree &
Evelyn stores, department
stores, boutiques, specialty
stores

Creighton's Naturally
11243-4 St. Johns Ind. Pkwy. S.
Jacksonville, FL 32246
904-642-4591
800-969-4591
Products: hair care, dandruff
shampoo, skin, toiletries,
bathing supply, deodorant,
soap, shaving supply
Availability: department
stores, discount department
stores, boutiques/specialty
stores, independent sales
representatives

Crème de la Terre
30 Cook Rd.
Stamford, CT 06902
203-324-4300
800-260-0700
Products: hypo-allergenic
skin care for men and
women, sun care, toiletries
Availability: health food
stores, boutiques, specialty
stores, mail order
MO

Crown Royale Ltd.
P.O. Box 5238
99 Broad St.
Phillipsburg, NJ 08865
908-859-6488
800-992-5400
Products: companion animal
care, fragrance for men and
women, household, carpet/
rug cleaning supply,
toiletries, shaving supply
Availability: grooming
shops, distributors
V MO

CYA Products, Inc.
6671 W. Indiantown Rd.
Suite 56-191
Jupiter, FL 33458
561-744-2998
cya@evcom.net
www.adzorbstar.com
Products: air freshener
Availability: health food
stores, companion animal
supply stores, distributors,
boutiques, specialty stores
V MO

Dallas Manufacturing Co.
4215 McEwen Rd.
Dallas, TX 75244
214-716-4200
800-256-8669
Products: companion animal care
Availability: discount department stores, supermarkets, companion animal supply stores, wholesale, mail order

Davidoff Fragrances
745 Fifth Ave., 10th Fl.
New York, NY 10151
212-850-2460
Products: Cool Water and Zino fragrances and ancillary products for men
Availability: department stores
V

Decleor USA, Inc.
18 E. 48th St., 21st Fl.
New York, NY 10017
212-838-1771
800-722-2219
Products: cosmetics, fragrance for men and women, hair care, dandruff shampoo, nail care, hypo-allergenic skin care for men and women, sun care, shaving supply, toiletries
Availability: department stores, boutiques, specialty stores, skin care salons, spas, Decleor stores

Deodorant Stones of America
9420 E. Doubletree Ranch Rd.
Suite C-101
Scottsdale, AZ 85258
602-451-4981
800-279-9318
dsa@priment.com
Products: deodorant stones
Availability: health food stores, department stores, supermarkets, drugstores, mail order
🖼 V MO

Dep Corporation
2101 E. Via Arado
Rancho Dominguez, CA 90220-6189
310-604-0777
Products: Dep hair care, LA Looks, Agree and Halsa hair care, Lavoris mouthwash, Topol tooth polish, Jordan toothbrushes, Cuticura toiletries, Porcelana fade cream, Nature's Family, Lilt
Availability: drugstores, supermarkets, discount department stores, department stores

Derma-E Skin & Hair Care
9400 Lurline Ave., Suite C-1
Chatsworth, CA 91311
818-718-1420
800-521-3342
Products: hair care, dandruff shampoo, hypo-allergenic skin care for men and women, shaving supply
Availability: health food stores, beauty supply stores, boutiques, specialty stores, mail order
MO

Dermalogica
1001 Knox St.
Torrance, CA 90502
310-352-4784
http://www.dermalogica.com
Products: aromatherapy, hair care, skin care, sun care
Availability: skin care salons

Dermatologic Cosmetic Laboratories
20 Commerce St.
East Haven, CT 06512
203-467-1570
800-552-5060
Products: baby care, hair care, dandruff shampoo, hypo-allergenic skin care for men and women, sun care, toiletries, cosmetics
Availability: doctors, aestheticians

Desert Essence
9510 Vassar Ave., Unit A
Chatsworth, CA 91311
818-709-5900
Products: toiletries, dental hygiene, hair care
Availability: health food stores

Desert Naturels, Inc.
74-940 Hwy. III, Suite 437
Indio, CA 92201
760-346-1604
800-243-4435
Products: hypo-allergenic skin care for men and women
Availability: health food stores, drugstores, distributors, cooperatives

DeSoto, Inc.
900 E. Washington St.
P.O. Box 609
Joliet, IL 60434
815-727-4931
800-544-2814
Products: private-label
household cleaning supply
Availability: supermarkets,
drugstores

Diamond Brands, Inc.
1660 S. Highway 100
Suite 590
Minneapolis, MN 55416
612-541-1500
Products: cosmetics, nail
care, La Salle "10" nail
treatments
Availability: drugstores,
discount department stores,
supermarkets

Dr. A. C. Daniels, Inc.
109 Worcester Rd.
Webster, MA 01570
508-943-5563
800-547-3760
Products: companion animal
care
Availability: department
stores, discount department
stores, drugstores,
independent sales representatives, companion animal
supply stores
MO

**Dr. Bronner's "All-One"
Products Company**
P.O. Box 28
Escondido, CA 92033-0028
760-743-2211
Products: castille soaps,
baby care, companion
animal care, hair care,
toiletries, health foods
Availability: health food
stores, cooperatives
V

**Dr. Hauschka Cosmetics
USA, Inc.**
59C North St.
Hatfield, MA 01038
800-247-9907
Products: holistic skin care,
hair care, cosmetics
Availability: health food
stores, cooperatives, salons,
boutiques

D.R.P.C. (AmerAgain)
567-1 S. Leonard St.
Waterbury, CT 06708
203-755-3123
Products: environmentally
friendly, recycled office
supply
Availability: office supply
stores, "green" stores
V

Earth Friendly Products
P.O. Box 607
Wood Dale, IL 60191-2688
800-335-3267
ecos@mcs.com
Products: household,
personal care
Availability: supermarkets,
health food stores, drug-
stores, mail order
MO

Earthly Matters
2950 St. Augustine Rd.
Jacksonville, FL 32207
904-398-1458
800-398-7503
Products: household, carpet/
rug cleaning supply, air
freshener, furniture polish,
laundry detergent
Availability: health food
stores, distributors
V MO

Earth Science, Inc.
23705 Via Del Rio
Yorba Linda, CA 92887
714-692-7190
800-222-6720
Products: hair care, hypo-
allergenic skin care, sun
care, toiletries, shaving
supply, fragrance for men
and women, dandruff
shampoo, nail care, baby
care
Availability: health food
stores, cooperatives, mail
order
MO

Earth Solutions, Inc.
1123 Zonolite Rd., #8
Atlanta, GA 30306
404-525-6167
800-883-3376
Products: natural hypo-
allergenic therapeutic skin
care for men, women, and
children, baby care, toiletries,
companion animal care
Availability: health food
stores, cooperatives,
boutiques, specialty stores,
independent sales representatives
V MO

**Eberhard Faber (Sanford
Corp.)**
2711 Washington Blvd.
Bellwood, IL 60104
708-547-5525
800-438-3703
Products: office supply
Availability: office supply
stores, drugstores, grocery
stores
MO

From the Earth.

Earth Friendly Products is a company committed to the environment. We

For the Earth.

provide our customers with household cleaning products that, without sacrificing cleaning power and value, are environmentally safe. No animal testing or ingredients are ever used.

Our product line is available at fine Natural Health Food stores, Super Markets and through the PETA Catalog.

Earth Friendly Products
P.O. Box 607
Wood Dale, IL 60191-2688

E. Burnham Cosmetics
7117 N. Austin Ave.
Niles, IL 60714
708-647-2121
Products: cosmetics, hypo-allergenic skin care for men and women, hair care
Availability: health food stores, drugstores, mail order
MO

Ecco Bella Botanicals
1133 Route 23
Wayne, NJ 07470
201-696-7766
Products: aromatherapy, cosmetics, fragrance for women, hair care, dandruff shampoo, household, air freshener, skin care, bathing supply, soap, shaving supply, toiletries
Availability: drugstores, health food stores, supermarkets, cooperatives, boutiques, specialty stores

Eco-Dent International, Inc.
P.O. Box 5285
Redwood City, CA 94063-3021
415-364-6343
Products: dental hygiene
Availability: drugstores, supermarkets, health food stores, dentists, cooperatives
MO

Eco Design Company
1365 Rufina Cir.
Santa Fe, NM 87501
505-438-3448
800-621-2591
Products: companion animal care, toiletries, air freshener, baby care, household, furniture polish, paint, wood finishing supply, art supply, toothbrushes, dental hygiene, hair care
Availability: health food stores, "eco" stores, mail order
MO

Ecover, Inc.
1072 S.E. Bristol St.
Suite 209
Santa Ana Heights, CA 92707
714-556-3644
Products: household, bleach
Availability: health food stores, supermarkets, cooperatives, mail order
MO

Edward & Sons Trading Company, Inc.
P.O. Box 1326
Carpinteria, CA 93014
805-684-8500
Products: household cleaning supply, health food, hair care
Availability: health food stores, cooperatives, boutiques, specialty stores, mail order
MO

27

Elizabeth Grady Face First
200 Boston Ave.
Suite 3500
Medford, MA 02155
617-391-9380
800-FACIALS
Products: cosmetics, hypo-
allergenic skin care for men
and women, sun care, nail
care, toiletries
Availability: Elizabeth Grady
Face First stores, distributors,
boutiques, specialty stores,
mail order
MO

**Elizabeth Van Buren
Aromatherapy**
P.O. Box 7542
303 Potrero St., #33
Santa Cruz, CA 95061
408-425-8218
800-710-7759
Products: aromatherapy,
fragrance for women, hypo-
allergenic skin care for
women, toiletries, bathing
supply, soap, essential oil
Availability: department
stores, drugstores, health
food stores, Elizabeth Van
Buren Aromatherapy stores,
metaphysical bookstores
V MO

Enfasi Hair Care
927 McGarry St.
Los Angeles, CA 90021
213-488-0777
Products: aromatherapy, hair
care, dandruff shampoo,
toiletries, cosmetics
Availability: beauty salons

English Ideas, Ltd.
15251 Alton Pkwy.
Irvine, CA 92618
714-789-8790
800-547-5278
Products: Advanced Lip
Technologies, personal care,
nonprescription therapy
Availability: beauty supply
stores, department stores,
salons

Epilady International, Inc.
c/o Beauty Care of America
39 Cindy La., Suite 300
Ocean, NJ 07712-7249
732-493-2435
800-879-LADY
Products: toiletries, Epilady
hair remover, facial saunas,
bath brushes, hair curlers,
companion animal care
Availability: drugstores,
department stores, discount
department stores, independent sales representatives
MO

Espial Corporation
7045 S. Fulton St., #200
Englewood, CO 80112-3700
303-799-0707
Products: household, hair
care, toiletries, skin care for
men and women
Availability: distributors,
mail order
V MO

Essential Aromatics
205 N. Signal St.
Ojai, CA 93023
805-640-1300
Products: aromatherapy, air
freshener, household, nail
care, skin care
Availability: health food
stores, cooperatives, mail
order
V MO

Essential Oil Company
P.O. Box 206
Lake Oswego, OR 97034
503-697-0615
Products: essential oil
Availability: health food
stores, mail order
MO

**Essential Products of
America, Inc.**
8702 N. Mobley Rd.
Odessa, FL 33556
813-877-9698
Products: essential oil,
vegetable oil, hypo-allergenic
skin care for men and
women, toiletries, fragrance
for men and women,
shaving supply, air freshener,
household
Availability: health food
stores, boutiques, specialty
stores, beauty salons, mail
order
V MO

Estée Lauder Inc.
767 Fifth Ave.
New York, NY 10153
212-572-4200
Products: cosmetics,
fragrance, nail care, skin
care, sun care, toiletries,
bathing supply, deodorant,
soap, shaving cream/lotion,
Clinique, Origins
Availability: department
stores, specialty stores

European Gold
33 S.E. 11th St.
Grand Rapids, MN 55744
218-326-0266
800-946-5395
Products: sun care, hypo-
allergenic skin care for men
and women
Availability: tanning salons,
beauty salons, fitness clubs
(where tanning beds are
used)

29

EuroZen
10 S. Franklin Tpk., #201
Ramsey, NJ 07446
201-447-0961
Products: aromatherapy,
scented massage oil, skin
care
Availability: independent
sales representatives, mail
order

Eva Jon Cosmetics
1016 E. California
Gainesville, TX 76240
817-668-7707
Products: cosmetics,
toiletries
Availability: health food
stores, spas, specialty shops,
mail order

Evans International
14 E. 15th St.
Richmond, VA 23224-0189
804-232-8946
800-368-3061
Products: office supply,
fingertip moistener, hand
lotion, janitorial cleaning
supply, household
Availability: office supply
stores, office supply catalogs

Legend

🖻 Company uses
Caring Consumer
product logo

V Vegan symbol
(products contain
no animal
ingredients

MO Mail order
available

Every Body, Ltd.
1738 Pearl St.
Boulder, CO 80302
303-440-0188
800-748-5675
Products: aromatherapy,
baby care, cosmetics, dental,
hair care, bathing supply,
massage oil, nail care, soap,
shaving supply, deodorant,
sun care, toiletries
Availability: Every Body,
Ltd., stores, mail order,
health food stores, supermarkets, cooperatives, bou-
tiques, sports industry stores
🖻 MO

Face Food Shoppe
21298 Pleasant Hill Rd.
Boonville, MO 65233
816-882-6858
800-882-6858
Products: cosmetics,
fragrances for women, hair
care, skin care for women,
toiletries, bathing supply,
soap
Availability: Face Food
Shoppe store, mail order
🖻 MO

Faces by Gustavo
P.O. Box 102-149
Arlington, VA 22201
703-908-9620
800-58-FACE
Products: aromatherapy,
baby care, cosmetics, hypo-
allergenic skin care, sun
care, toiletries, soap
Availability: Faces by
Gustavo stores, boutiques,
specialty stores, salons, mail
order
🖻 MO

**Facets/Crystalline Cosmet-
ics, Inc.**
8436 N. 80th Place
Scottsdale, AZ 85258
602-991-1704
Products: skin care for men
and women
Availability: mail order
MO

Faith Products, Ltd.
Unit 5, Kay St.
Bury Lancashire BL9 6BU
England
161-7642555
Products: laundry detergent,
dandruff shampoo, soap,
skin care, hair care,
fragrance for men and
women, baby care, shaving
supply, aromatherapy,
deodorant
Availability: health food
stores, mail order
MO

**Farmavita USA (Chuckles,
Inc.)**
P.O. Box 5126
Manchester, NH 03109
603-669-4228
800-221-3496
Products: hair color
Availability: salons

Faultless Starch/Bon Ami
510 Walnut St.
Kansas City, MO 64106-
1209
816-842-1230
Products: household
cleaning supply
Availability: grocery stores,
drugstores

Fernand Aubry
14, rue Alexandre Parodi
75010 Paris
France
1-42-05-83-79
Products: cosmetics,
fragrance for men and
women, nail care, skin care
for men and women,
toiletries
Availability: department
stores, selected spas and
salons, boutiques, specialty
stores

Finelle Cosmetics
137 Marston St.
Lawrence, MA 01841-2297
800-733-9889
Products: cosmetics,
fragrance for men and
women, hair care, skin care
for men and women, sun
care, toiletries
Availability: distributors,
salons, mail order
MO

**Fleabusters/Rx For Fleas,
Inc.**
6555 N.W. Ninth Ave.
Suite 412
Ft. Lauderdale, FL 33309
954-351-9244
800-666-3532
Products: Fleabusters
companion animal care, Rx
For Fleas Plus powder
Availability: mail order,
veterinarians
MO

**Flower Essences of Fox
Mountain**
P.O. Box 381
Worthington, MA 01098
413-238-4291
Products: vibrational
medicine, holistic health
care, nonperscription
therapy
Availability: health food
stores, bookstores, mail
order
V MO

Focus 21 International
2755 Dos Aarons Way
Vista, CA 92083
619-727-6626
800-832-2887
Products: hair care
Availability: salons

Food Lion
P.O. Box 1330
Salisbury, NC 28145-1330
704-633-8250
Products: personal care,
household
Availability: Food Lion stores

Forest Essentials
2144 Colorado Ave.
Santa Monica, CA 90404
800-301-7767
Products: fragrance for
women, hair and skin care
for men and women, sun
care, toiletries, body and
skin care gifts
Availability: environmental
product stores, beauty
supply stores, gift shops,
department stores, catalogs
MO

Forever Living Products
P.O. Box 29041
Phoenix, AZ 85038
602-998-8888
Products: hair care,
toiletries, dental hygiene,
companion animal care,
household, carpet/rug
cleaning supply, skin care
for men and women, sun
care, nutritional beverages
Availability: distributors
MO

**Forever New International,
Inc.**
4701 N. Fourth Ave.
Sioux Falls, SD 57104-0403
605-331-2910
800-456-0107
Products: soap for fine
washables, household
Availability: department
stores, specialty stores,
boutiques, mail order
V MO

**For Pet's Sake Enterprises,
Inc.**
3780 Eastway Rd., Suite 10A
South Euclid, OH 44118
216-932-8810
800-285-0298
Products: aromatherapy,
baby care, cosmetics,
fragrance, hair care, dandruff
shampoo, household, nail
care, skin care, toiletries,
vitamins, deodorant, car
care
Availability: mail order
MO

Fort Howard Corporation
1919 S. Broadway
P.O. Box 19130
Green Bay, WI 54307-9130
414-435-8821
Products: recycled paper
products Envision, Soft 'n
Gentle, So-Dri
Availability: grocery stores,
natural food stores

IV Trail Products
P.O. Box 1033
Sykesville, MD 21784
410-795-8989
Products: companion animal
care for horses
Availability: mail order

Fragrance Impressions, Ltd.
116 Knowlton St.
Bridgeport, CT 06608
203-367-6995
800-541-3204
Products: fragrance for men
and women
Availability: drugstores,
supermarkets

Framesi USA, Inc.
400 Chess St.
Coraopolis, PA 15108
412-269-2950
800-321-9648
Products: hair care, hair
color, permanents
Availability: salons

Legend

🖼 Company uses
Caring Consumer
product logo

V Vegan symbol
(Products contain
no animal
ingredients)

MO Mail order
available

Frank T. Ross & Sons, Ltd.
(Nature Clean)
6550 Lawrence Ave. E.
Scarborough
Ontario M1C 4A7
Canada
416-282-1107
Products: household, bleach,
oven cleaner, laundry soap,
dish soap, hair care,
toiletries, laundry
Availability: health food
stores, cooperatives, mail
order
V MO

Freeda Vitamins, Inc.
36 E. 41st St.
New York, NY 10017
212-685-4980
800-777-3737
Products: vitamins and
nutrients
Availability: health food
stores, drugstores, cooperatives, Freeda Vitamin stores,
mail order
Note: 20 percent discount to
PETA members
V MO

**Freeman Cosmetic
Corporation**
10000 Santa Monica Blvd.
#400
Los Angeles, CA 90067
310-286-0101
mail.freeman.com
Products: hair care, skin and
bath care for men and
women, sun care
Availability: drugstores,
supermarkets, beauty supply
stores

Free Spirit Enterprises, Inc.
P.O. Box 2638
Guerneville, CA 95446
707-869-1942
Products: personal care
Availability: health food
stores, cooperatives,
drugstores, specialty stores,
mail order
V MO

Frontier Cooperative Herbs
3021 78th St.
Box 299
Norway, IA 52318
319-227-7996
800-669-3275
Products: aromatherapy,
fragrance, household,
baking
soda, toiletries, bathing
supply, soap
Availability: drugstores,
health food stores,
cooperatives, mail order
V MO

Fruit of the Earth, Inc.
P.O. Box 152044
Irving, TX 75015-2044
972-790-0808
800-527-7731
Products: sun care, skin
care, hair care
Availability: drugstores,
supermarkets, discount
department stores

Garden Botanika
8624 154th Ave. N.E.
Redmond, WA 98052
206-881-9603
800-968-7842
Products: baby care,
cosmetics, fragrance, hair
care, nail care, skin care,
sun care, toiletries, bathing
supply, deodorant, soap,
shaving supply
Availability: Garden
Botanika stores, mail order

Garnier (L'Oréal)
575 Fifth Ave.
New Yorkn NY 10017
212-818-1500
Products: hair color
Availability: supermarkets,
drugstores
Note: Garnier does not test
its products on animals. It
may, however, test its
ingredients on animals.

Georgette Klinger, Inc.
501 Madison Ave.
New York, NY 10022
212-838-3200
800-KLINGER
Products: cosmetics,
fragrance for men and
women, hair care, nail care,
skin care, sun care,
toiletries, bathing supply,
soap, shaving supply
Availability: Georgette
Klinger salons, specialty
stores, mail order

Gigi Laboratories
2220 Gaspar Ave.
Los Angeles, CA 90040
213-728-2999
Products: skin care for
women
Availability: boutiques,
specialty stores, beauty
supply stores

Giovanni Cosmetics, Inc.
5415 Tweedy Blvd.
Southgate, CA 90280
213-563-0355
Products: hair care
Availability: health food
stores, salons, boutiques,
specialty stores, mail order
MO

Golden Pride/Rawleigh, Inc.
1501 Northpoint Pkwy.
Suite 100
West Palm Beach, FL 33407
407-640-5700
Products: household,
furniture polish, laundry
detergent, vitamins
Availability: distributors,
mail order
MO

**Goldwell Cosmetics (USA),
Inc.**
981 Corporate Blvd.
Linthicum, MD 21090
301-725-6620
800-288-9118
Products: hair care, hair
color
Availability: salons

Green Ban
P.O. Box 146
Norway, IA 52318
319-446-7495
Products: insect-bite
treatment, companion
animal care, baby care,
body and massage oil,
toiletries, shaving supply
Availability: health food
stores, cooperatives, mail
order

Green Earth Office Supply
P.O. Box 719
Redwood Estates, CA 95044
800-327-8449
geo7@ix.netcom.com
http://www/welcom.com/geos/
Products: office supply, glue,
hemp, art supply
Availability: mail order
MO

Greentree Laboratories, Inc.
P.O. Box 425
Tustin, CA 92681
714-546-9520
Products: companion animal
care
Availability: companion
animal supply stores, mail
order
MO

Greenway Products
P.O. Box 183
Port Townsend, WA 98368
206-385-7124
800-966-1445
Products: household,
toiletries, companion animal
care, hair care, carpet/rug
cleaning supply, hypo-
allergenic skin care for men
and women, shaving supply,
accessories and promotional
items
Availability: distributors,
mail order
V MO

Gryphon Development
767 Fifth Ave.
New York, NY 10153-0038
212-582-1220
Products: Victoria's Secret,
Bath & Body Works,
Abercrombie & Fitch,
Henri Bendel, toiletries,
personal care, fragrance
Availability: stores named
above

Gucci Parfums
15 Executive Blvd.
Orange, CT 06477
203-787-4711
800-243-5555
Products: fragrance for men
and women, toiletries,
shaving supply, skin care
Availability: department
stores

Halo Purely for Pets
3438 E. Lake Rd., #14
Palm Harbor, FL 34685
813-854-2214
Products: companion animal supplements, skin treatments, foods
Availability: companion animal supply stores, health food stores, mail order
MO

Halston Borghese, Inc.
767 Fifth Ave., 49th Fl.
New York, NY 10153-0002
212-572-3100
Products: fragrance for men and women, Princess Marcella Borghese cosmetics
Availability: department stores, beauty supply stores

Hard Candy, Inc.
110 N. Doheny Dr.
Beverly Hills, CA 90211
310-275-8099
Products: cosmetics, nail care
Availability: department stores, boutiques

Hargen Distributing, Inc.
4015 N. 40th Place
Phoenix, AZ 85018
602-381-0799
Products: deodorant stones
Availability: health food stores, mail order
V MO

Legend

🛏 Company uses Caring Consumer product logo

V Vegan symbol (products contain no animal ingredients)

MO Mail order available

34

Harvey Universal Environmental Products
15948 Downey Ave.
Paramount, CA 90723
310-328-9000
800-800-3330
Products: household and industrial cleaning supply, carpet/rug cleaning, air freshener
Availability: health food stores, distributors, companion animal supply stores, supermarkets, cooperatives, boutiques, specialty stores, home centers, mail order
V MO

Healthy Times
461 Vernon Way
El Cajon, CA 92020
619-593-2229
Products: baby care
Availability: health food stores, cooperatives, mail order, select baby stores
V MO

Helen Lee Skin Care and Cosmetics
205 E. 60th St.
New York, NY 10022
212-888-1233
800-288-1077
Products: toiletries, sun care, hair care, cosmetics, nail care, hypo-allergenic skin care for men and women, essential oil, theatrical makeup, fragrance for women
Availability: salons, Helen Lee Day Spa, distributors, mail order
MO

Henri Bendel
712 Fifth Ave.
New York, NY 10019
212-247-1100
Products: fragrance for women
Availability: Henri Bendel stores, mail order
MO

Herbal Products & Development
P.O. Box 1084
Aptos, CA 95001
408-688-8706
Products: vitamins, whole food and herbal concentrates
Availability: health food stores, camping stores, cooperatives, independent sales representatives, mail order
MO

Herb Garden
P.O. Box 773
Pilot Mountain, NC 27041
910-368-2723
Products: aromatherapy, fragrance, companion animal care, personal care
Availability: mail order, farmers' market
V MO

H.e.r.c. Consumer Products
2538 N. Sandy Creek Dr.
Westlake Village, CA 91361
818-991-9985
Products: household
Availability: health food stores, home and hardware stores, mail order
V MO

Heritage Store, Inc.
P.O. Box 444
Virginia Beach, VA 23458
757-428-0100
800-862-2923
Products: dental hygiene, fragrance for men and women, hair care, dandruff shampoo, hypo-allergenic skin care for men and women, toiletries, health care items, sun care
Availability: health food stores, Heritage Store, mail order
MO

Hewitt Soap Company, Inc.
333 Linden Ave.
Dayton, OH 45403
513-253-1151
800-543-2245
Products: companion animal care, fragrance for men and women, toiletries
Availability: health food stores, drugstores, department stores, discount department stores, boutiques, specialty stores, distributors, mail order
MO

Hobé Laboratories, Inc.
4032 E. Broadway
Phoenix, AZ 85040
602-257-1950
800-528-4482
Products: hair care, skin care for men and women, hair loss and scalp problem shampoo, psoriasis treatment, supplements, weight loss tea, topical analgesic
Availability: health food stores, drugstores, mail order, salons, chiropractors
MO

Homebody (Perfumoils, Inc.)
143A Main St.
Brattleboro, VT 05301
802-254-6280
Products: toiletries, fragrance for men and women, shaving supply, hypoallergenic skin care for men and women, glycerin soaps, hair care
Availability: Homebody stores

Home Health Products, Inc.
P.O. Box 8425
Virginia Beach, VA 23450
757-468-3130
800-284-9123
Products: aromatherapy, cosmetics, dental, hair care, dandruff shampoo, household, air freshener, nail care, skin care, toiletries, vitamins, bathing supply, deodorant, soap
Availability: health food stores, cooperatives, mail order
MO

Home Service Products Company
P.O. Box 245
Pittstown, NJ 08867
908-735-5988
Products: Professional Brand, laundry detergent, bleach, household
Availability: independent sales representatives, mail order

House of Cheriss
13475 Holiday Dr.
Saratoga, CA 95070
408-867-6795
Products: ayurvedic skin care for women and men, cleansing cream, washing grains, toner, moisturizer, body lotion, hair oil, travel packs
Availability: health food and specialty stores in San Francisco Bay area, mail order
MO

H2O Plus, Inc.
845 W. Madison
Chicago, IL 60607
312-850-9283
800-242-BATH
Products: skin care for men and women, shaving supply, sun care, hair care, cosmetics, fragrance for men and women, baby and child care, nail care, toothbrushes, toys
Availability: H2O Plus stores, department stores, duty-free shops, boutiques, specialty stores, mail order
MO

Huish Detergents, Inc.
3540 W. 1987 S.
P.O. Box 25057
Salt Lake City, UT 84125
801-975-3100
800-776-6702
Products: household, private label household, all-fabric bleach
Availability: department stores, discount department stores, drugstores, supermarkets, cooperatives

Ida Grae (Nature's Colors Cosmetics)
424 La Verne Ave.
Mill Valley, CA 94941
415-388-6101
Products: cosmetics, hypoallergenic skin care for men and women, *Nature's Colors: Dyes From Plants* (book)
Availability: i natural stores, health food stores, specialty stores, boutiques, cooperatives, mail order
MO

Il-Makiage
107 E. 60th St.
New York, NY 10022
212-371-3992
800-722-1011
Products: cosmetics, hair
care, hair color, nail care,
hypo-allergenic skin care
for women
Availability: cooperatives, Il-
Makiage stores, boutiques,
specialty stores, salons,
health spas, mail order

Ilona Inc.
3201 E. Second Ave.
Denver, CO 80206
303-322-3000
Products: cosmetics
Availability: department stores

Image Laboratories, Inc.
2340 Eastman Ave.
Oxnard, CA 93030
805-988-1767
800-421-8528
Products: hair care, dandruff
shampoo, hair color,
permanents
Availability: salons

**i natural cosmetics
(Cosmetic Source)**
32-02 Queen's Blvd.
Long Island City, NY 11101
718-729-2929
800-962-5387
Products: cosmetics,
toiletries, hair care, hypo-
allergenic skin care for
men and women, sun
care, shaving supply
Availability: i natural
stores, General Nutrition
Centers

Innovative Formulations, Inc.
1810 S. Sixth Ave.
S. Tucson, AZ 85713
520-628-1553
Products: paint, coatings
for roof, household,
roofing material, architec-
tural paint, nail polish
remover
Availability: mail order
V MO

Legend

🛏 Company uses
Caring Consumer
product logo
V Vegan symbol
(products contain
no animal
ingredients)
MO Mail order
available

International Rotex, Inc.
P.O. Box 20697
Reno, NV 89515
702-356-8356
800-648-1871
Products: office supply, correction fluid
Availability: discount department stores, drugstores, supermarkets, cooperatives, wholesale distributors

International Vitamin Corporation
209 40th St.
Irvington, NJ 07111
201-371-7300
Products: vitamins
Availability: health food stores, mail order
MO

InterNatural
1100 Lotus Dr.
Silver Lake, WI 53170
414-889-8501
800-548-3824
Products: cosmetics, toiletries, household, oil, candles, incense
Availability: mail order
MO

IQ Products Company
16212 State Hwy. 249
Houston, TX 77086
713-444-6454
Products: hair care, insect repellent, car care, cleaning supply
Availability: discount stores, drugstores, grocery stores

Jacki's Magic Lotion
258 A St., #7A
Ashland, OR 97520
503-488-1388
Products: skin care for men and women, massage lotion
Availability: health food stores, massage product retailers, health spas, cooperatives, mail order
MO

James Austin Company (Austin Diversified)
P.O. Box 827
115 Downieville Rd.
Mars, PA 16046
412-625-1535
800-245-1942
Products: laundry detergent, bleach, carpet/rug cleaning supply, household
Availability: supermarkets, department stores, discount department stores, drugstores, mail order
Note: no catalog
MO

Jason Natural Cosmetics
8468 Warner Dr.
Culver City, CA 90232-2484
310-838-7543
800-527-6605
Products: toiletries, hair care, hypo-allergenic skin care for men and women, sun care, shaving supply
Availability: health food stores, drugstores, cooperatives, boutiques, specialty stores, mail order
MO

J.C. Garet, Inc.
2471 Coral St.
Vista, CA 92083
619-598-0505
800-548-9770
Products: household cleaning supply, laundry soap
Availability: department stores, supermarkets, drugstores, health food stores, cooperatives, boutiques, uniform stores, distributors
MO

Jeanne Rose Aromatherapy
219 Carl St.
San Francisco, CA 94117-3804
415-564-6785
Products: aromatherapy, companion animal care, hypo-allergenic skin care for men and women, toiletries, herbs, oil
Availability: health food stores, cooperatives, boutiques, specialty stores, independent sales representatives, mail order
MO

Jessica McClintock, Inc.
1400 16th St.
San Francisco, CA 94103-5181
415-495-3030
800-333-5301
Products: Jessica McClintock fragrance for women, Scott McClintock fragrance for men, toiletries, shaving supply
Availability: department stores, specialty stores, Jessica McClintock, boutiques, mail order

Jheri Redding (Conair Corporation)
1 Cummings Point Rd.
Stamford, CT 06904
203-351-9000
800-7-CONAIR
Products: hair care, permanents, toiletries, Conair hair care styling tools
Availability: drugstores, supermarkets, beauty supply stores, discount department stores

Joe Blasco Cosmetics
7340 Greenbriar Pkwy.
Orlando, FL 32819
407-363-7070
800-553-1520
Products: cosmetics, skin care, theatrical makeup and supply
Availability: salons, mail order

John Amico Expressive Hair Care Products
4731 W. 136th St.
Crestwood, IL 60445
708-598-7800
800-676-5264
Products: hair care, dandruff shampoo, permanents, hair coloring, toiletries, bathing supply, soap, shaving supply
Availability: salons, mail order

John Paul Mitchell Systems
26455 Golden Valley Rd.
Santa Clarita, CA 91350
805-298-0400
800-321-JPMS
Products: hair care, permanents, skin care, sun care
Availability: salons

JOICO Laboratories, Inc.
P.O. Box 42308
Los Angeles, CA 90042-0308
818-968-6111
800-44-JOICO
http://www.joico.com
Products: hair care, hair color, permanents, skin care, toiletries, bathing supply
Availability: salons, beauty supply stores

Jolen Creme Bleach, Inc.
25 Walls Dr.
P.O. Box 458
Fairfield, CT 06430
203-259-8779
Products: Jolen Creme Bleach for facial and body hair
Availability: supermarkets, drugstores, discount department stores

J.R. Liggett, Ltd.
R.R. 2, Box 911
Cornish, NH 03745
603-675-2055
shampoo@cyberportal.net
Products: hair care, dandruff shampoo
Availability: health food stores, cooperatives, boutiques, specialty stores, independent sales representatives, mail order

Jurlique Cosmetics
1000 Holcombe Woods Pkwy., Suite 318
Roswell, GA 30076
770-643-6999
800-854-1110
Products: sun care, baby care, toiletries, household, hair care, dandruff oils, cosmetics
Availability: salons, spas, mail order

Katonah Scentral
51 Katonah Ave.
Katonah, NY 10536
914-232-7519
800-29-SCENT
Products: toiletries, hair care, shaving supply, fragrance for men and women, essential oil, baby care, dental hygiene, toothbrushes, hair color, aromatherapy
Availability: Katonah Scentral stores, mail order

K.B. Products, Inc.
20 N. Railroad Ave.
San Mateo, CA 94401
415-344-6500
800-342-4321
Products: companion animal care, hair care, dandruff shampoo, hand lotion
Availability: companion animal supply stores, groomers, K.B. stores, mail order

Kenic Pet Products, Inc.
109 S. Main St.
Lawrenceburg, KY 40342
800-228-7387
Products: companion animal care
Availability: companion animal supply stores, grooming stores, hardware stores, cooperatives, boutiques, specialty stores, mail order

Ken Lange No-Thio Permanent Waves & Hair
7112 N. 15th Place, Suite 1
Phoenix, AZ 85020
800-486-3033
Products: hair care, permanents
Availability: salons

Kenra Laboratories, Inc.
6501 Julian Ave.
Indianapolis, IN 46219
317-356-6491
.800-428-8073
Products: hair care, skin care
Availability: salons

Kimberly Sayer, Inc.
125 W. 81st St., #2A
New York, NY 10024
212-362-2907
Products: hypo-allergenic skin care for men and women, toiletries
Availability: distributors, boutiques, specialty stores, mail order
MO

Kiss My Face
P.O. Box 224
144 Main St.
Gardiner, NY 12525
914-255-0884
800-262-KISS
Products: hair care, skin care for men and women, sun care, cosmetics, toiletries, shaving supply, baby care
Availability: health food stores, drugstores, cooperatives, boutiques, massage therapists, salons, mail order
MO

Kleen Brite Laboratories, Inc.
200 State St.
Brockport, NY 14602
716-637-0630
800-223-1473
Products: household, bleach, laundry detergents
Availability: drugstores, supermarkets

KMS Research, Inc.
4712 Mountain Lakes Blvd.
Redding, CA 96003
916-244-6000
800-DIAL-KMS
Products: hair care, dandruff shampoo, permanents
Availability: salons

Natural Personal Care Products   PO Box 224, Gardiner, NY 12525

KSA Jojoba
19025 Parthenia St., #200
Northridge, CA 91324
818-701-1534
Products: cosmetics,
fragrance for men and
women, hair care, nail care,
hypo-allergenic skin care for
men and women, shaving
supply, toiletries, companion
animal care, baby care
Availability: mail order

La Costa Products International
2875 Loker Ave. E.
Carlsbad, CA 92008
619-438-2181
800-LA-COSTA
Products: cosmetics, hair
care, nail care, skin care for
women, sun care, shaving
supply, toiletries
Availability: salons, mail
order
MO

La Crista, Inc.
P.O. Box 240
Davidsonville, MD 21035
410-956-4447
800-888-2231
Products: hypo-allergenic
skin care for men and
women, baby care,
toiletries, massage oil
Availability: health food
stores, drugstores, supermarkets, boutiques, specialty
stores, Walmart, mail order
[symbols] V MO

L'anza Research International, Inc.
935 W. Eighth St.
Azusa, CA 91702
818-334-9333
800-423-0307
Products: hair care, dandruff
shampoo, permanents, hair
color
Availability: salons
V

LaNatura
425 N. Bedford Dr.
Beverly Hills, CA 90210
310-271-5616
800-352-6288
Products: baby care,
fragrance for women,
toiletries, candles, body
care, bathing supply, soap
Availability: health food
stores, LaNatura stores,
boutiques, specialty stores,
hotel private label, mail
order
V MO

Lander Company, Inc.
106 Grand Ave.
Englewood, NJ 07631
201-568-9700
Products: personal care for
consumer and institutional use
Availability: retail stores,
distributors

La Prairie, Inc.
31 W. 52nd St.
New York, NY 10019
212-459-1600
800-821-5718
Products: skin care for
women, sun care, cosmetics,
fragrance for women
Availability: department
stores, specialty stores,
boutiques

Lee Pharmaceuticals
1434 Santa Anita Ave.
South El Monte, CA
91733
818-442-3141
800-950-5337
Products: Lee acrylic nails
and nail care, Nose Better,
Zip hair removal, Saxon
after shave cream, Sundance
aloe, Peterson's ointment,
Creamalin antacid, Bikini
Bare depilatory
Availability: drugstores,
grocery stores, boutiques

Levlad/Nature's Gate Herbal Cosmetics
9200 Mason Ave.
Chatsworth, CA 91311
818-882-2951
800-327-2012
Products: dental hygiene,
toiletries, sun care, hypo-allergenic skin care for men
and women, dandruff
shampoo, soap, deodorant,
bathing supply
Availability: health food
stores, drugstores, cooperatives, mail order

Liberty Natural Products, Inc.
8120 S.E. Stock St.
Portland, OR 97215
503-256-1227
800-289-8427
Products: baby care, air
freshener, dental hygiene,
sun care, toothbrushes,
toiletries, fragrance for
women, skin care, household
Availability: health food
stores, cooperatives
V

From nature without cruelty.

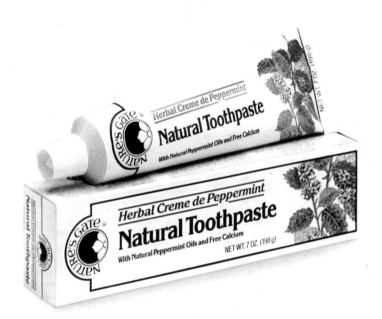

Life Dynamics, Inc.
21640 N. 19th Ave.
Suite C101
Phoenix, AZ 85027
602-582-5977
800-977-9664
Products: hair care, hypo-allergenic skin care for men and women, toiletries, natural color protection
Availability: distributors, specialty stores, mail order

Life Tree Products
P.O. Box 513
Graton, CA 95444
707-588-0755
Products: household, dishwashing, laundry, all-purpose cleaning supply, toiletries, liquid soap
Availability: health food stores, supermarkets, camping stores, mail order, drugstores
V MO

Lightning Products
1900 Erie St.
N. Kansas City, MO 64116
816-221-3183
Products: companion animal care, household, carpet/rug cleaning supply
Availability: companion animal supply stores, health food stores, mail order
MO

Lily of Colorado
P.O. Box 12471
Denver, CO 80212
303-455-4194
Products: purely botanical skin care
Availability: health food stores, mail order
MO

Lime-O-Sol Company (The Works)
P.O. Box 395
Ashley, IN 46705
219-587-9151
Products: household cleaning supply, drain opener
Availability: supermarkets, drugstores, department stores

Lissée Cosmetics
927 McGarry St.
Los Angeles, CA 90021
213-488-0777
Products: cosmetics, aromatherapy, skin care for women, hair care, dandruff shampoo, sun care
Availability: drugstores, beauty supply stores, boutiques, specialty stores
V

Liz Claiborne Cosmetics, Inc.
1441 Broadway
New York, NY 10018
212-354-4900
Products: fragrance for men and women, toiletries, shaving supply, bathing supply, deodorant, soap
Availability: department stores, Liz Claiborne stores

Lobob Laboratories
1440 Atteberry La.
San Jose, CA 95131-1410
408-432-0580
800-83LOBOB
Products: hard and soft lens cleaner, wetting solution, soaking solution
Availability: mail order, grocery stores, drugstores
V MO

Logona USA, Inc.
554-E Riverside Dr.
Asheville, NC 28801
704-252-1420
Products: hair care, baby care, dental hygiene, hypo-allergenic skin care for men and women, hair color, sun care, fragrance for men, toiletries, shaving supply, dandruff shampoo
Availability: health food stores, cooperatives, boutiques, specialty stores, mail order
MO

L'Oréal (Cosmair)
575 Fifth Ave.
New York, NY 10017
212-818-1500
Products: cosmetics, hair care, fragrance for men and women, hair color, nail care, permanents, hypo-allergenic skin care for men and women, toiletries
Availability: department stores, drugstores, supermar-kets, boutiques, specialty stores, discount department stores
Note: L'Oréal does not test its products on animals. It may, however, test its ingredients on animals.

Lotus Light
1100 Lotus Dr.
Silver Lake, WI 53170
414-889-8501
800-548-3824
Products: cosmetics, household, air freshener, baby care, fragrance for men and women, hair care, dandruff shampoo, hair color, dental hygiene, toothbrushes, hypo-allergenic skin care
Availability: drugstores, health food stores, cooperatives, mail order

Louise Bianco Skin Care, Inc.
13655 Chandler Blvd.
Sherman Oaks, CA 91401
818-786-2700
800-782-3067
Products: hypo-allergenic skin care for men and women, sun care, toiletries
Availability: mail order, salons
MO

M.A.C. Cosmetics
100 Alden Rd.
Markham, Ontario L3R 4C1
Canada
416-924-0598
800-387-6707
Products: cosmetics, hypo-allergenic skin care for men and women, nail care, hair care, theatrical makeup
Availability: department stores, M.A.C. Cosmetics stores

Magick Botanicals
3412 W. MacArthur Blvd., #K
Santa Ana, CA 92704
714-957-0674
800-237-0674
Products: hair care, skin care for men and women, toiletries, baby care
Availability: health food stores, mail order
MO

Magic of Aloe
7300 N. Crescent Blvd.
Pennsauken, NJ 08110
609-662-3334
800-257-7770
Products: cosmetics, hair care, skin care for men and women, sun care, toiletries, shaving supply
Availability: health food stores, boutiques, specialty stores, Value Vision Home Shopping, distributors, mail order
MO

Mallory Pet Supplies
118 Atrisco Dr. S.W.
Albuquerque, NM 87105
505-836-4033
800-824-4464
Products: companion animal care
Availability: companion animal supply stores, mail order
MO

Marcal Paper Mills, Inc.
1 Market St.
Elmwood Park, NJ 07407
201-796-4000
www.marcalpaper.com
Products: recycled household paper, toilet paper
Availability: supermarkets, drugstores
V

Marché Image Corporation
P.O. Box 1010
Bronxville, NY 10708
914-793-2093
800-753-9980
cmarch4416@aol.com
Products: skin care for men and women, tanning cream, household, carpet/rug cleaning supply
Availability: distributors, mail order
MO

Marilyn Miglin Institute
112 E. Oak St.
Chicago, IL 60611
312-943-1120
800-662-1120
Products: skin care, cosmetics, fragrance for women and men
Availability: Marilyn Miglin Institute, sales consultants, mail order
MO

Martin Von Myering
422 Jay St.
Pittsburgh, PA 15212
412-766-3186
Products: skin care, hair care, permanents, hair color
Availability: health food stores, salons, mail order
V MO

Masada Marketing Company
P.O. Box 4767
N. Hollywood, CA 91617-0767
818-503-4611
800-368-8811
Products: Dead Sea mineral bath salts
Availability: health food stores, cooperatives, mail order

Mastey de Paris, Inc.
25413 Rye Canyon Rd.
Valencia, CA 91355
805-257-4814
800-6-MASTEY
Products: hair care, sun care, hair color, toiletries, hypo-allergenic skin care for men and women, permanents, dandruff shampoo
Availability: salons, beauty schools, mail order
MO

Maybelline, Inc. (L'Oréal)
P.O. Box 372
Memphis, TN 38101-0372
901-324-0310
800-944-0730
Products: cosmetics
Availability: grocery stores, drugstores
Note: Maybelline was purchased by L'Oréal in 1996. It does not test its products or ingredients on animals.

Mehron, Inc.
100 Red Schoolhouse Rd.
Chestnut Ridge, NY 10977
914-426-1700
800-332-9955
Products: theatrical makeup, cosmetics
Availability: boutiques, specialty stores, party supply and costume stores, mail order
MO

Melaleuca, Inc.
3910 S. Yellowstone Hwy.
Idaho Falls, ID 83402-6003
208-522-0700
Products: household, toiletries, sun care, feminine hygiene care, hair care, fragrance for men and women, hypo-allergenic skin care, dental hygiene, cosmetics, companion animal care
Availability: independent sales representatives, mail order
Note: In 1996, in the course of litigation, Melaleuca commissioned an LD50 test on a competitor's product, resulting in the suffering and deaths of 10 rats. Melaleuca has provided PETA with a letter renewing its commitment to a non-animal-testing policy.
MO

Mère Cie, Inc.
1100 Soscol Rd., #3
Napa, CA 94558
707-257-8510
800-832-4544
merecie@napanet.net
Products: fragrance for men and women
Availability: health food stores, drugstores, cooperatives, supermarkets, mail order
MO

Merle Norman
9130 Bellanca Ave.
Los Angeles, CA 90045
213-641-3000
Products: cosmetics, skin care
Availability: Merle Norman salons

Mia Rose Products, Inc.
177-F Riverside Ave.
Newport Beach, CA 92663
714-662-5465
800-292-6339
Miarose@ix.netcom.com
Products: household, aromatherapy
Availability: health food stores, boutiques, cooperatives, drugstores, specialty stores, mail order, supermarkets, distributors
MO

Michael's Health Products
6820 Alamo Downs Pkwy.
San Antonio, TX 78238
210-647-4700
800-525-9643
Products: vitamins, herbs
Availability: health food stores

Michelle Lazar Cosmetics
755 South Lugo Ave.
San Bernardino, CA 92048
909-888-6310
800-676-8008
Products: skin care
Availability: health food stores, mail order
MO

Micro Balanced Products
25 Aladdin Ave.
P.O. Box 8
Dumont, NJ 07628
201-387-0200
800-626-7888
Products: hypo-allergenic skin care for men and women, sun care, toiletries
Availability: health food stores, mail order
V MO

Mira Linder Spa in the City
29935 Northwestern Hwy.
Southfield, MI 48034
313-356-5810
800-321-8860
Products: cosmetics, hypo-allergenic skin care for men and women, nail care
Availability: Mira Linder Spa in the City stores, mail order
MO

Montagne Jeunesse
The Old Grain Store
4 Denne Rd.
Horsham, W. Sussex Rh12 1JE
England
1403-272 737
Products: skin care for women, hair care, toiletries, gift sets, soaps, hand/body lotion
Availability: department stores, supermarkets, boutiques, specialty stores

Monteil Paris (Lancaster Group USA)
745 Fifth Ave.
New York, NY 10151
212-593-7400
Products: cosmetics, skin care for men and women, fragrance for women, nail care
Availability: department stores, specialty stores

Mother's Little Miracle, Inc.
930 Indian Peak Rd.
Suite 215
Rolling Hills Estates, CA 90274
310-544-7125
Products: baby care, children's stain and odor remover and prewash, spit-up remover, air freshener
Availability: drugstores, discount department stores, boutiques, specialty stores, distributors, mail order
V MO

Mountain Ocean Ltd.
5150 Valmont Rd.
Boulder, CO 80306
303-444-2781
Products: baby care (prenatal), hair care, toiletries
Availability: health food stores, supermarkets, mail order
MO

Mr. Christal's
1100 Glendon Ave.
Suite 1250
Los Angeles, CA 90024
310-824-2508
800-426-0108
Products: companion animal care
Availability: companion animal supply stores, veterinarians

Nadina's Cremes
3600 Clipper Mill Rd.
Suite 140
Baltimore, MD 21211
410-235-9192
800-722-4292
Products: scented body
creme for men and women,
body care
Availability: health food
stores, drugstores, cooperatives, boutiques, specialty
stores, independent sales
representatives, environmental stores, New Age stores,
mail order

Nala Barry Labs
P.O. Box 151
Palm Desert, CA 92261
619-321-7098
800-397-4174
Products: companion animal
care, nutritional supplements
Availability: health food
stores, cooperatives,
boutiques, garden shops,
companion animal supply
stores, specialty stores
V MO ⬛

Narwhale of High Tor, Ltd.
591 S. Mountain Rd.
New City, NY 10956
914-634-8832
800-354-2407
Products: cosmetics, hypo-
allergenic skin care for men
and women, sun care
Availability: mail order
MO

Natracare
191 University Blvd.
Suite 294
Denver, CO 80206
303-320-1510
Products: feminine hygiene
Availability: drugstores,
health food stores, cooperatives, boutiques, specialty
stores, mail order
V MO

Naturade Cosmetics
7110 E. Jackson St.
Paramount, CA 90723
310-531-8120
800-421-1830
Products: hair care, hypo-
allergenic skin care for men
and women, dandruff
shampoo, toiletries, baby
care, companion animal
care, cosmetics
Availability: health food
stores, cooperatives,
supermarkets, boutiques,
specialty stores, mail order
⬛ MO

**Natural Animal Health
Products, Inc.**
7000 U.S. 1 N.
St. Augustine, FL 32095
904-824-5884
800-274-7387
Products: skin care for
animals, Earth-safe household
and yard supply
Availability: health food
stores, lawn and garden
stores, cooperatives,
companion animal supply
stores, veterinarians,
groomers

Natural Bodycare, Inc.
355 N. Lantana St.
Camarillo, CA 93011
805-445-9237
Products: hair care,
toiletries, skin care,
fragrance for women, sun
care, dandruff shampoo,
household
Availability: health food
stores, mail order
V MO

Natural Chemistry, Inc.
244 Elm St.
New Canaan, CT 06840
203-966-8761
800-753-1233
Products: pool supply,
household, companion
animal care
Availability: health food
stores, cooperatives,
environmental product
stores, mail order
MO

**Naturally Free, The Herbal
Alternative**
R.R. 1, Box 4753
Charlotte, VT 05445
802-985-5601
Products: herbal insect
repellent for home, people,
and companion animals
Availability: health food
stores, cooperatives, sporting
goods stores, veterinarians,
environmentally friendly
stores, mail order
V MO

Naturally Yours, Alex
P.O. Box 3398
Holiday, FL 34690-0398
813-443-7479
Products: companion animal
care
Availability: health food
stores, companion animal
supply stores, mail order,
holistic veterinarians
V MO

47

Natural Products Company
7782 Newburg Rd.
Newburg, PA 17240-9601
717-423-5818
800-323-0418
Products: companion animal care
Availability: health food stores, gift stores, companion animal supply stores

Natural Research People, Inc.
South Route, Box 12
Lavina, MT 59046
406-575-4343
Products: companion animal care
Availability: health food stores, veterinarians, companion animal supply stores, cooperatives, mail order

Natural Science
41 Madison Ave., 4th Fl.
New York, NY 10010
212-725-7661
888-EARTHSAFE
Products: hair care, fragrance for men and women, hypo-allergenic skin care, aromatherapy, baby care, cosmetics, sun care
Availability: health food stores, department stores, drugstores, mail order

Natural (Surrey)
13110 Trails End Rd.
Leander, TX 78641
512-267-7172
Products: toiletries, shaving supply, soap
Availability: health food stores, drugstores, department stores, supermarkets, mail order

Natural Therapeutics Centre
2500 Side Cove
Austin, TX 78704
512-444-2862
Products: mustard seed bath
Availability: health food stores, mail order

Natural Touch
P.O. Box 2894
Kirkland, WA 98083-2894
206-820-2788
Products: cosmetics
Availability: department stores

Natural World, Inc.
7373 N. Scottsdale Rd.
Suite A-280
Scottsdale, AZ 85251
602-905-1110
Products: hair care, household, companion animal care, sun care, hypo-allergenic skin care for men and women, shaving supply, baby care, dental hygiene, furniture polish, toiletries, air freshener
Availability: distributors, mail order

Nature de France, Ltd. (Para Laboratories)
100 Rose Ave.
Hempstead, NY 11550
516-538-4600
800-645-3752
Products: toiletries, deodorant, soap
Availability: department stores, discount department stores, drugstores, health food stores, supermarkets, cooperatives, boutiques, specialty stores, mail order

Nature's Acres
8984 E. Weinke Rd.
North Freedom, WI 53951
608-522-4492
Products: cosmetics, soap, toner, body oil
Availability: health food stores, mail order

Nature's Best (Natural Research People)
South Route, Box 12
Lavina, MT 59046
406-575-4343
Products: companion animal care
Availability: companion animal supply stores, health food stores, mail order

Nature's Country Pet
1765 Garnet Ave., Suite 12
San Diego, CA 92109
619-230-1058
800-576-PAWS
Products: companion animal care
Availability: health food stores, companion animal supply stores, mail order

Nature's Plus
548 Broadhollow Rd.
Melville, NY 11747-3708
516-293-0030
800-645-9500
Products: dietary supplements, hair care, nail care,
skin care for men and
women, toiletries, cosmetics
Availability: health food
stores

Nectarine
1200 Fifth St.
Berkeley, CA 94710
510-528-0162
Products: aromatherapy,
toiletries, shaving supply,
hair care, fragrance for men
and women, massage oil
and lotion, skin care for men
and women
Availability: private label for
drugstores, health food
stores, boutiques, specialty
stores, bath and fragrance
stores

Nemesis, Inc.
4525 Hiawatha Ave.
Minneapolis, MN 55406
612-724-5732
800-340-4898
Products: hair care, dandruff
shampoo, companion
animal care
Availability: beauty supply
stores, boutiques, specialty
stores, mail order
 MO

Legend
 Company uses
Caring Consumer
product logo
V Vegan symbol
(Products contain
no animal
ingredients)
MO Mail order
available

Neocare Laboratories, Inc.
3333 W. Pacific Coast Hwy.,
4th Fl.
Newport Beach, CA 92663
800-982-4NEO
Products: hypo-allergenic
skin care for men and
women, household, pool
and spa supply, odor
eliminator, grease trap and
septic tank control
supply
Availability: health food
stores, cooperatives, mail
order
 V MO

New Age Products
16200 N. Hwy. 101
Willits, CA 95490-9710
707-459-5969
Products: household
Availability: health food
stores
V

Neway
Little Harbor
Marblehead, MA 01945
617-631-9400
Products: household
Availability: health food
stores, mail order
V MO

Neways, Inc.
150 E. 400 N.
Salem, UT 84653
801-423-2800
800-998-7233
Products: cosmetics, hair
care, hypo-allergenic skin
care for men and women,
sun care, toiletries, shaving
supply, dental hygiene,
household, nail care
Availability: distributors,
boutiques, specialty stores,
mail order
MO

New Moon Extracts, Inc.
99 Main St.
P.O. Box 1947
Brattleboro, VT 05301
802-257-0018
800-543-7279
Products: skin care,
nutritional supplements,
herbal extracts, ginger
delivery system
Availability: health food
stores, cooperatives, doctors,
aestheticians, mail
order
V MO

Nexxus Products Company
82 Coromar Dr.
Santa Barbara, CA 93116
805-968-6900
Products: hair color, hair
care, permanents, vitamins,
toiletries, dandruff shampoo
Availability: salons

Nirvana, Inc.
P.O. Box 18413
Minneapolis, MN 55418
612-932-2919
800-432-2919
Products: hair care, skin care
Availability: drugstores,
health food stores, mail
order
V MO

No Common Scents
Kings Yard
220 Xenia Ave.
Yellow Springs, OH 45387
513-767-4261
800-686-0012
Products: fragrance for men
and women, air freshener,
companion animal care,
incense, bath crystals
Availability: No Common
Scents store, mail order
MO

Nordstrom
865 Market St.
San Francisco, CA 94103
410-243-8500
800-7-BEAUTY
Products: Nordstrom Bath Ltd. (bath and body care), Simple and Natural Essentials (skin care and makeup), Nordstrom Essentials (bath and body care), Single Notes (fragrance)
Availability: Nordstrom department stores, mail order

Norelco
1010 Washington Blvd.
P.O. Box 120015
Stamford, CT 06912-0015
203-973-0200
Products: electric razors
Availability: department stores, drugstores, supermarkets
V

North Country Soap
7888 County Rd., #6
Maple Plain, MN 55359
612-479-3381
800-667-1202
Products: baby care, companion animal care, insect repellant, hypo-allergenic skin care, sun care, toiletries, bathing supply, deodorant, soap
Availability: drugstores, health food stores, North Country Soap stores, boutiques, specialty stores, independent sales representatives, mail order, museum gift shops, resorts, hotels, sports shops
MO

N/R Laboratories, Inc.
900 E. Franklin St.
Centerville, OH 45459
513-433-9570
800-223-9348
Products: companion animal care
Availability: distributors, mail order
MO

NuSkin International, Inc.
One NuSkin Plaza
Provo, UT 84601
801-377-6056
800-366-6875
Products: hair care, skin care for men and women, sun care, toiletries, nutritional supplements
Availability: distributors, mail order
MO

NutriBiotic
865 Parallel Dr.
Lakeport, CA 95453
707-263-0411
800-225-4345
Products: dental hygiene, nutritional supplements, toiletries
Availability: health food stores

Nutri-Cell, Inc. (Derma-Glo)
1038 N. Tustin, Suite 309
Orange, CA 92667-5958
714-953-8307
Products: companion animal care, hypo-allergenic skin care for men and women, sun care
Availability: health food stores, drugstores, supermarkets, cooperatives, mail order
V MO

Nutri-Metics International, USA, Inc.
12723 E. 166th St.
Cerritos, CA 90703
310-802-0411
Products: cosmetics, toiletries, household
Availability: distributors
MO

Nutrina Company, Inc.
1117 Foothill Blvd.
La Canada, CA 91011
818-790-1776
800-523-8899
Products: vitamins
Availability: health food stores, cooperatives

Oasis Biocompatible Products
1020 Veronica Springs Rd.
Santa Barbara, CA 93105-4532
805-682-3449
Products: household, laundry detergent, all-purpose cleaning supply
Availability: health food stores, cooperatives, Real Goods catalog
V MO

Ohio Hempery, Inc.
7002 S.R. 329
Guysville, OH 45735
614-662-4367
800-BUY-HEMP
Products: cosmetics, skin care for men and women, clothing, hemp paper
Availability: health food stores, mail order
MO

Oil of Orchid
P.O. Box 1040
Guerneville, CA 95446
707-869-0761
Products: skin care for men
and women
Availability: health food
stores, cooperatives, mail
order
V MO

Oliva Ltd.
P.O. Box 4387
Reading, PA 19606
610-779-7854
Products: toiletries
Availability: cooperatives,
health food stores, mail
order
V MO

OPI Products, Inc.
13034 Saticoy St.
N. Hollywood, CA 91605
818-759-2400
800-341-9999
opinails@aol.com
Products: nail care
Availability: beauty salons,
professional beauty supply
stores

Orange-Mate
P.O. Box 883
Waldport, OR 97394
503-563-3290
800-626-8685
Products: air freshener
Availability: department
stores, discount department
stores, drugstores, health
food stores, cooperatives,
specialty stores, independent
sales representatives
V MO

**Organic Moods (KMS
Research, Inc.)**
4712 Mountain Lakes
Blvd.
Redding, CA 96003
916-244-6000
800-DIAL-KMS
Products: hypo-allergenic
skin care for men and
women, toiletries
Availability: salons

Oriflame Corporation
76 Treble Cove Rd.
N. Billerica, MA 01862
508-663-2700
800-959-0699
Products: toiletries, hypo-
allergenic skin care for men
and women, sun care,
cosmetics, fragrance for men
and women, hair care,
vitamins
Availability: distributors,
mail order
MO

**Origins Natural Resources
(Estée Lauder)**
767 Fifth Ave.
New York, NY 10153
212-572-4100
Products: sensory therapy,
cosmetics, skin care for men
and women, fragrance, sun
care, toiletries, bathing
supply, soap, shaving supply,
vegan makeup brushes
Availability: department
stores, Origins stores,
boutiques, specialty stores

Orjene Natural Cosmetics
5-43 48th Ave.
Long Island City, NY 11101
718-937-2666
800-886-7536
Products: cosmetics,
toiletries, shaving supply,
skin care for men and
women, sun care, hair care
Availability: health food
stores, cooperatives, mail
order
MO

Orlane
555 Madison Ave.
New York, NY 10022
212-750-1111
800-535-368
Products: cosmetics,
fragrance for women, sun
care
Availability: department
stores, drugstores, boutiques,
specialty stores, distributors

Orly International, Inc.
9309 Deering Ave.
Chatsworth, CA 91311
818-998-1111
800-275-1111
Products: aromatherapy, nail
care, skin care for women
Availability: drugstores,
supermarkets, salons, beauty
supply stores

Otto Basics—Beauty 2 Go!
P.O. Box 9023
Rancho Santa Fe, CA 92067
619-756-2026
800-598-OTTO
Products: cosmetics
Availability: department
stores, QVC television,
direct TV marketing
MO

Legend

🖼 Company uses
Caring Consumer
product logo

V Vegan symbol
(products contain
no animal
ingredients)

MO Mail order
available

Oxyfresh U.S.A., Inc.
E. 12928 Indiana Ave.
P.O. Box 3723
Spokane, WA 99220
509-924-4999
Products: dental hygiene, hair care, air freshener, skin care for men and women, toiletries, companion animal care, household, toothbrushes, nutrition
Availability: distributors, mail order
V MO

Pacific Scents, Inc.
P.O. Box 8205
Calabasas, CA 91375-8205
818-999-0832
800-554-7236
Products: essential oil, toiletries, audiocassettes with subliminal affirmations
Availability: health food stores, mail order
V MO

Pangea
7829 Woodmont Ave.
Bethesda, MD 20814
301-652-3181
pangeaveg@aol.com
Products: skin care, hair care, deodorant, dental supply, shaving supply, feminine hygiene, baby care, companion animal care
Availability: Pangea store, mail order
V MO

Parfums Houbigant Paris
1135 Pleasant View Terr. W.
Ridgefield, NJ 07657
201-941-3400
Products: fragrance for men and women, toiletries, skin care for men and women
Availability: department stores, boutiques, specialty stores, mail order
MO

Park Rand Products Company
P.O. Box 1111
Los Angeles, CA 90028-1111
818-362-6218
Products: household
Availability: drugstores, supermarkets, mail order
V MO

Parlux Fragrances, Inc.
3725 S.W. 30th Ave.
Ft. Lauderdale, FL 33312
954-316-9008
800-727-5895
Products: cosmetics, fragrance for women and men
Availability: department stores and drugstores

Pathmark Stores, Inc.
301 Blair Rd.
Woodbridge, NJ 07095
908-499-3000
Products: dental, toothbrushes, baking soda, razors, vitamins, air freshener
Availability: Pathmark supermarkets and drugstores in Conn., N.J., N.Y., Pa., and Del.

Patricia Allison Natural Beauty Products
4470 Monahan Rd.
La Mesa, CA 91941
619-444-4163
800-858-8742
Products: cosmetics, fragrance for women, hypoallergenic skin care, sun care, toiletries, bathing supply, soap, massage oil
Availability: mail order
MO

Paul Mazzotta, Inc.
P.O. Box 96
Reading, PA 19607
610-376-2250
800-562-1357
Products: cosmetics, hair care, dandruff shampoo, hair color, permanents, hypoallergenic skin care for men and women, sun care, toiletries
Availability: salons, Paul Mazzotta stores
 V MO

Paul Penders Company, Inc.
1340 Commerce St.
Petaluma, CA 94954
707-763-5828
800-440-7285
Products: cosmetics, hair care, hair color, hypoallergenic skin care, toiletries, bathing supply, shaving supply
Availability: health food stores, mail order
MO

Peaceable Kingdom
1902 W. Sixth St.
Wilmington, DE 19805
302-429-8687
Products: cosmetics, toiletries, household cleaning supply, laundry, baby care, recycled paper
Availability: mail order, Peaceable Kingdom store
MO

52

Perfect Balance Cosmetics, Inc.
2 Ridgewood Rd.
Malvern, PA 19355-9629
610-647-7780
Products: thigh-smoothing cream, cosmetics, hypoallergenic skin care for men and women, hair care, fragrance for men and women, sun care
Availability: distributors, salons, health spas and clubs, independent sales representatives, mail orde
MO

The Pet Connection
P.O. Box 391806
Mountain View, CA 94039
415-949-1190
Products: companion animal care, carpet-cleaning supply
Availability: companion animal stores, mail order, department stores, drugstores, health food stores, cooperatives
MO

PetGuard, Inc.
165 Industrial Loop S.
Unit 5
Orange Park, FL 32073
904-264-8500
800-874-3221
Products: companion animal care
Availability: health food stores, companion animal supply stores, veterinary offices, environmental product stores, cooperatives

Pets 'n People, Inc.
(Nature's Miracle)
930 Indian Peak Rd.,
Suite 215
Rolling Hills Estates, CA 90274
310-544-7125
Products: companion animal cleaning supply, litter treatment, carpet/rug-cleaning supply
Availability: companion animal supply stores, distributors, mail order
V MO

Pharmagel Corporation
P.O. Box 50531
Santa Barbara, CA 93150
800-882-4889
Products: skin care
Availability: health food stores, mail order
MO

Pilot Corporation of America
60 Commerce Dr.
Trumbull, CT 06611
203-377-8800
Products: office supply, writing instruments
Availability: office supply stores, grocery stores, drugstores, catalogs
V

Planet, Inc.
10114 McDonald Park Rd.
C-16, R.R. 3
Sidney, B.C. V8L 3X9
Canada
604-656-9436
Products: household
Availability: health food stores, cooperatives, grocery stores, mail order
V MO

PlantEssence Natural Body Care
P.O. Box 14743
Portland, OR 97293-0743
503-281-4147
800-752-6898
plantessence.com/~patrick
Products: air freshener, body oil, lip balm, fragrance for men and women, toiletries, skin care for men and women, mouth freshener
Availability: health food stores, cooperatives, boutiques, specialty stores, mail order
MO

Potions & Lotions—Body and Soul, Inc.
10201 N. 21st Ave., #8
Phoenix, AZ 85021
602-944-6642
800-456-3765
Products: aromatherapy, fragrance for men and women, hair care, sun care, hypo-allergenic skin care for men and women, shaving supply, air freshener, toothbrushes, toiletries, baby care
Availability: health food stores, boutiques, specialty stores, Potions & Lotions stores, mail order
 MO

Prescription Plus Clinical Skin Care
25028 Kearny Ave.
Valencia, CA 91355
800-877-4849
Products: skin care for men and women, sun care
Availability: professional skin care salons and clinics, day spas, doctors

Prescriptives, Inc. (Estée Lauder)
767 Fifth Ave.
New York, NY 10153
212-572-4400
Products: cosmetics, fragrance for women, skin care, sun care, toiletries, bathing supply, soap
Availability: department stores, specialty stores

Prestige Cosmetics
1330 W. Newport Center Dr.
Deerfield Beach, FL 33442
305-480-9202
800-722-7488
Products: cosmetics, nail care
Availability: drugstores, supermarkets, boutiques, specialty stores, beauty supply stores

Prestige Fragrances Ltd. (Revlon)
625 Madison Ave.
New York, NY 10022
212-572-5000
Products: fragrance for women
Availability: department stores

Principal Secret (Guthy Renker Corporation)
41-550 Ecclectic St., Suite 200
Palm Desert, CA 92260
800-545-5595
Products: skin care for men and women
Availability: J.C. Penney, home shopping networks, mail order
MO

Professional Choice Hair Care
2937 S. Alameda St.
Los Angeles, CA 90058
310-277-3974
800-326-3974
Products: hair care
Availability: beauty supply stores

Professional Pet Products, Inc.
1873 N.W. 97th Ave.
Miami, FL 33172
305-592-1992
800-432-5349
Products: companion animal care
Availability: companion animal supply stores, cooperatives, drugstores
V MO

Pro-Ma Systems
477 Commerce Way, #113
Longwood, FL 32750
407-331-1133
Products: cosmetics, hair care, nail care, sun care, toiletries, deodorant, soap, shaving supply, vitamins, fuel additives, fuel lubricant, car care
Availability: independent sales representatives, mail order
MO

Pro-Tan (Green Mountain)
P.O. Box 51867
Bowling Green, KY 42101
502-796-8353
Products: sun care
Availability: health food stores, drugstores, department stores, cooperatives, mail order
V MO

Pro-Tec Pet Health
2395-A Monument Blvd.
Concord, CA 94520
510-676-9600
800-44-FLEAS
Products: companion animal care
Availability: companion animal supply stores, health food stores, groomers, feed stores, mail order
MO

P.S.I. Industries, Inc.
1619 Shenandoah Ave.
P.O. Box 4391
Roanoke, VA 24017
703-345-5013
Products: industrial odor/stain remover
Availability: distributors, mail order
MO

Pulse Products
2021 Ocean Ave., #105
Santa Monica, CA 90405
310-399-3447
310-392-0991
Products: massage oil
Availability: health food stores
V MO

Pure & Basic Products
20600 Belshaw Ave.
Carson, CA 90746
310-898-1630
800-432-3787
Products: hair care, toiletries, bathing supply, deodorant, soap, shaving supply, skin care, dandruff shampoo, air freshener, household, hypo-allergenic skin care for women and men
Availability: salons, beauty supply stores, cooperatives, mail order
V MO

Indulge Yourself Naturally with ...

- Japanese Green Tea
- All Natural Colors
- Botanical Extracts
- Alpha-Hydroxy Acids
- Competitively Priced
- pH Balanced

PURE & BASIC

For free samples and complete information call
1-800-432-3787

Pure Touch Therapeutic Body Care
P.O. Box 1281
Nevada City, CA 95959
916-265-5949
800-442-PURE
Products: fragrance for women, spa supply for massage professionals
Availability: health food stores, spas, distributors
V MO

Quan Yin Essentials
P.O. Box 2092
Healdsburg, CA 95448
707-431-0529
Products: fragrance for men and women, toiletries, skin care for men and women
Availability: health food stores, department stores, boutiques, specialty stores, gift stores, independent sales representatives
V MO

Queen Helene
100 Rose Ave.
Hempstead, NY 11550
516-538-4600
800-645-3752
Products: hair care, dandruff shampoo, skin care, toiletries, bathing supply, deodorant, soap
Availability: department stores, discount department stores, drugstores, health food stores, supermarkets, cooperatives, boutiques, specialty stores
MO

Rachel Perry, Inc.
9111 Mason Ave.
Chatsworth, CA 91311
818-888-5881
800-624-7001
Products: skin care, sun care, cosmetics
Availability: health food stores, beauty supply stores, Rachel Perry stores in Los Angeles, mail order
MO

Legend
🖼 Company uses Caring Consumer product logo
V Vegan symbol (products contain no animal ingredients
MO Mail order available

55

Rainbow Research Corporation
170 Wilbur Place
Bohemia, NY 11716
516-589-5563
800-722-9595
Products: baby care, hair care, hair color, hypoallergenic skin care, toiletries, bathing supply, soap
Availability: drugstores, health food stores, cooperatives, boutiques, specialty stores, mail order

Rainforest Company
701 N. 15th St., Suite 500
St. Louis, MO 63103
314-621-1330
Products: aromatherapy, hair care, toiletries, bathing supply, soap, rain forest-derived gifts
Availability: health food stores, boutiques, specialty stores

Ranir/DCP Corporation
4701 E. Paris
S.E. Grand Rapids, MI 49512
616-698-8880
Products: toothbrushes, dental floss
Availability: health food stores, drugstores, supermarkets, department stores
V

Real Animal Friends
101 Albany Ave.
Freeport, NY 11520
516-223-7600
Products: companion animal care
Availability: companion animal supply stores, discount department stores, boutiques, specialty stores, mail order
V MO

Legend
 Company uses Caring Consumer product logo
V Vegan symbol (products contain no animal ingredients)
MO Mail order available

Redken Laboratories, Inc.
(L'Oréal)
575 Fifth Ave.
New York, NY 10017
212-818-1500
800-423-5369
Products: hair care, hair color, permanents, dandruff shampoo, hypo-allergenic skin care for men and women, toiletries, shaving supply, cosmetics, fragrance for women
Availability: salons
Note: Redkin does not test its products on animals. It may, however, test its ingredients on animals.

Redmond Products, Inc.
18930 W. 78th St.
Chanhassen, MN 55317
612-934-4868
800-328-0159
Products: hair care, Aussie, VitaMend
Availability: grocery stores, drugstores, beauty supply stores

Rely Enterprises Corp.
7 Stonebridge Ct.
Manalapan, NJ 07726
908-780-1378
Products: Rely all-purpose cleaner concentrate
Availability: mail order
🗒 V MO

Reviva Labs, Inc.
705 Hopkins Rd.
Haddonfield, NJ 08033
609-428-3885
800-257-7774
Products: cosmetics, baby care, hair care, dandruff shampoo, sun care, hypo-allergenic skin care for men and women, toiletries, shaving supply
Availability: health food stores, drugstores, discount department stores, supermarkets, cooperatives, boutiques, distributors, mail order
MO

Revlon, Inc.
625 Madison Ave.
New York, NY 10022
212-572-5000
Products: cosmetics, toiletries, hair color, hair care, nail care, Almay, Jean Naté, Flex, Outrageous, Ultima II
Availability: drugstores, department stores, supermarkets, beauty supply stores, discount department stores

Royal Laboratories
2849 Dundee Rd., Suite 112
Northbrook, IL 60062
800-876-9253
Products: vitamins
Availability: health food stores, cooperatives
V MO

Royal Labs Natural Cosmetics
Box 22434
Charlesston, SC 29413
803-552-1504
800-203-5151
Products: Chemical-free cosmetics, hypo-allergenic skin care for men and women, sun care, toiletries, hair care, aromatherapy
Availability: health food stores, skin clinics, beauty salons, boutiques, spas, specialty stores, mail order
V MO

Rusk, Inc.
One Cummings Point Rd.
Stamford, CT 06904
203-316-4300
800-829-7875
Products: hair care
Availability: salons

Safeway, Inc.
Fourth & Jackson sts.
Oakland, CA 94660
510-891-3000
Products: household, toiletries, baby care, toothbrushes
Availability: Safeway supermarkets

Sagami, Inc.
825 North Cass Ave., Suite 101
Westmont, IL 60559
708-789-9999
Products: condoms (Excalibur, Sagami Type E, Vis-à-Vis, Peace & Sound regular, Peace & Sound ultra thin)
Availability: supermarkets, drugstores, specialty stores
V

Sanford Corporation
2711 Washington Blvd.
Bellwood, IL 60104
708-547-5525
800-438-3703
Products: office supply
Availability: office supply
stores, drugstores, grocery
stores, mail order
MO

**San Francisco Soap
Company**
1129 Industrial Ave., Suite 200
Petaluma, CA 94975-0428
707-769-5120
Products: skin care,
toiletries, bathing supply,
soap
Availability: department
stores, health food stores,
drugstores, supermarkets,
cooperatives mail order
MO

**Santa Fe Botanical
Fragrances, Inc.**
P.O. Box 282
Santa Fe, NM 87504
505-473-1717
perfume@NewMexico.com
Products: botanical
colognes, fragrance for men
and women, aromatherapy
Availability: mail order
V MO

Santa Fe Soap Company
369 Montezuma, #167
Santa Fe, NM 87501
505-757-6764
Products: hair care, toiletries
Availability: health food
stores, bath shops, bou-
tiques, supermarkets,
cooperatives, specialty
stores, mail order
V MO

Sappo Hill Soapworks
654 Tolman Creek Rd.
Ashland, OR 97520
503-482-4485
Products: soap
Availability: health food
stores
V

Schiff Products, Inc.
1960 S. 4250 W.
Salt Lake City, UT 84104
801-972-0300
Products: vitamin/mineral
supplements
Availability: health food
stores, mail order
MO

Scruples, Inc.
8231 214th St. W.
Lakeville, MN 55044
612-469-4646
Products: hair care, hair
coloring,
Availability: beauty salons

Sea-renity
c/o Israel Business Centers
Tel-Aviv Hilton, Indepen-
dence Park
Tel-Aviv, Israel 63405
972-3-520-22
Products: aromatherapy, skin
and spa care for men and
women, bath salts, Dead Sea
black mud body wraps,
holistic scrubs, shower gel,
soap
Availability: health food
stores, cooperatives,
boutiques, specialty stores,
distributors
MO

Sebastian International, Inc.
6109 DeSoto Ave.
Woodland Hills, CA 91367
818-999-5112
800-829-7322
Products: hair care, hair
color, skin care for women
Availability: salons, Sebastian
collective salon members

SerVaas Laboratories
P.O. Box 7008
1200 Waterway Blvd.
Indianapolis, IN 46207
317-636-7760
800-433-5818
Products: household
Availability: supermarkets,
discount department stores,
drugstores

Seventh Generation
One Mill St.
Burlington, VT 05401-1530
802-658-3773
800-456-1177
Products: baby care, bleach,
feminine hygiene, house-
hold, laundry detergent
Availability: health food
stores, mail order, supermarkets
V MO

Shadow Lake, Inc.
P.O. Box 2597
Danbury, CT 07813-2597
203-778-0881
800-343-6588
Products: household, air
freshener, carpet cleaning
supply, toiletries, soap
Availability: discount
department stores, drug-
stores, health food stores,
supermarkets, cooperatives,
boutiques, specialty stores,
mail order
MO

Shahin Soap Company
427 Van Dyke Ave.
Haledon, NJ 07508
201-790-4296
Products: soap
Availability: mail order
V MO

Shene Cosmetics
22761 Pacific Coast Hwy.,
Suite 264
P.O. Box 2206
Malibu, CA 90265
800-315-1967
Products: sun protection
cosmetics, nail care,
toiletries
Availability: discount
department stores, mail order
MO

Shikai (Trans-India Products)
P.O. Box 2866
Santa Rosa, CA 95405
707-544-0298
800-448-0298
Products: hair care, hair
styling, hand and body
lotion, shower and bath gel
for men and women, color-
enhancing shampoo
Availability: health food
stores, drugstores, cooperatives, salons, mail order
MO

Shirley Price Aromatherapy
P.O. Box 65
Pineville, PA 18946
215-598-3802
Products: hypo-allergenic
skin care for men and
women, pure essential oil of
therapeutic quality
Availability: massage
therapists, salons, spas,
health food stores, mail
order
MO

**Shivani Ayurvedic Cosmet-
ics (Devi, Inc.)**
P.O. Box 377
Lancaster, MA 01523
508-368-0066
800-237-8221
Products: aromatherapy,
cosmetics, fragrance, hair
care, skin care, toiletries,
soap
Availability: health food
stores, cooperatives, mail
order
MO

**Simplers Botanical
Company**
P.O. Box 39
Forestville, CA 95436
707-887-2012
800-6JASMIN
Products: aromatherapy,
companion animal care,
herbal extracts, personal
care
Availability: mail order,
health food stores
🖼 V MO

Simple Wisdom, Inc.
775 S. Graham
Memphis, TN 38111
901-458-4686
800-370-6550
Products: toiletries, hair
care, skin care for men and
women, massage oil,
perfume oil, essential oil,
fragrance for women,
household, liquid soap, spot
remover
Availability: health food
stores, cooperatives,
boutiques, specialty stores,
mail order
MO

Sinclair & Valentine
480 Airport Blvd.
Watsonville, CA 95076-
2056
408-722-9526
Products: aromatherapy,
baby care, household, air
freshener, skin care for
women, toiletries, bathing
supply, soap
Availability: discount
department stores, drug-
stores, health food stores,
supermarkets

**Sirena (Tropical Soap
Company)**
P.O. Box 112220
Carrollton, TX 75011
214-357-1464
800-527-2368
Products: Sirena liquid and
bar soaps
Availability: health food
stores, mail order
V MO

Smith & Vandiver
480 Airport Blvd.
Watsonville, CA 95076-
2056
408-722-9526
Products: aromatherapy,
baby care, cosmetics,
fragrance for women, hair
care, household, air
freshener, razors, skin care,
sun care, toiletries, bathing
supply, soap, shaving supply,
home fragrance, candles
Availability: department
stores, health food stores,
Smith & Vandiver stores,
boutiques, specialty stores

SoapBerry Shop Company
50 Galaxy Blvd., Unit 12
Rexdale, Ont. M9W 4Y5
Canada
416-213-0802
Products: hair care, sun
care, cosmetics, tooth-
brushes, baby care, hypo-
allergenic skin care for men
and women, toiletries,
shaving supply, dental
hygiene, fragrance for men
and women, nail care
Availability: SoapBerry Shop
stores, mail order
MO

**Sojourner Farms Natural Pet
Products**
11355 Excelsior Blvd.
Hopkins, MN 55343
888-867-6567
holistic@visi.com
Products: natural companion
animal care, food, and
supply
Availability: health food
stores, cooperatives,
companion animal supply
stores, mail order
MO

Solgar Vitamin Company
500 Willow Tree Rd.
Leonia, NJ 07605
201-944-2311
Products: vitamins
Availability: health food
stores, cooperatives

Sombra Cosmetics, Inc.
5600-G McLeod N.E.
Albuquerque, NM 87109
505-888-0288
800-225-3963
Products: cosmetics, hair
care, hypo-allergenic skin
care for men and women,
sun care, theatrical makeup
Availability: health food
stores, mail order

Song of Life
152 Fayette St.
Buckhannon, WV 26201
304-472-6114
Products: Abby's comfrey
goldenseal salve (skin care
for men, women, babies,
and animals)
Availability: health food
stores, cooperatives,
boutiques, specialty stores,
natural food and herb
wholesalers, mail order
MO

SoRik International
278 Taileyand Ave.
Jacksonville, FL 32202
904-353-4200
800-940-HAIR
Products: hair care, sun care,
toiletries
Availability: salons
MO

Soya System, Inc.
1572 Page Industrial Ct.
St. Louis, MO 63132
314-428-0004
Products: hair care,
permanents
Availability: salons, beauty
supply stores

**Spa Natural Beauty
Products**
1201 16th St., #212
Denver, CO 80202
800-598-3878
Products: cosmetics, hypo-
allergenic skin care for men
and women, sun care,
toiletries, hair care,
fragrance for women
Availability: Spa Natural
Beauty Products stores, mail
order
MO

Spanish Bath
P.O. Box 750428
Petaluma, CA 94975-0428
707-769-5120
Products: toiletries, bath gel,
body lotion, mineral salt
Availability: discount
department stores, cooperatives, health food stores,
drugstores, boutiques,
specialty stores, mail order
V MO

Staedtler, Ltd.
Cowbridge Rd.
Pontyclym, Mid Glamorgan
Wales
0448 237421
Products: writing instru-
ments, office supply
Availability: office supply
stores in the U.K.

Stanhome, Inc.
50 Payson Ave.
Easthampton, MA 01027-
2262
413-527-4001
Products: household
Availability: hardware stores,
distributors

Stature Field Corporation
1143 Rockingham Dr.
Suite 106
Richardson, TX 75080
214-644-7000
800-348-3600
Products: razors, blades
Availability: health food
stores, cooperatives, mail
order
V MO

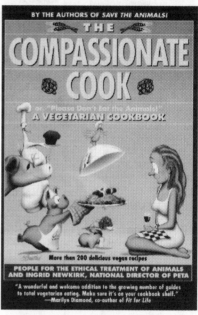

Steps in Health, Ltd.
P.O. Box 1409
Lake Grove, NY 11755
516-471-2432
800-471-8343
Products: companion animal
care, dental hygiene, hair
care, household, air
freshener, skin care for
women, toiletries, deodorant, soap, vitamins
Availability: mail order
MO

**Stevens Research Salon
Products**
19417 63rd Ave. N.E.
Arlington, WA 98223
360-435-4513
800-262-3344
Products: hair care
Availability: salons, beauty
schools
V

Studio Magic, Inc.
20135 Cupress Creek Dr.
Alva, FL 33990-3305
941-728-3344
800-749-5002
Products: cosmetics, hypo-
allergenic skin care for men
and women, sun care,
theatrical makeup
Availability: Studio Magic
stores, boutiques, specialty
stores, independent sales
representatives, doctors,
salons, mail order
MO

Sukesha (Chuckles, Inc.)
P.O. Box 5126
Manchester, NH 03109
603-669-4228
800-221-3496
Products: hair care, hair
color, permanents
Availability: salons

Sumeru
P.O. Box 2110
Freedom, CA 95019
408-722-4104
800-478-6378
Products: aromatherapy,
baby care, personal care
Availability: health food
stores, mail order
V MO

**SunFeather Herbal Soap
Company**
1551 Highway 72
Potsdam, NY 13676
315-265-3648
800-771-7627
Products: soap-making
supply, personal care
Availability: health food
stores, department stores,
gift stores, boutiques, mail
order
V MO

Sunrider International
1625 Abalone Ave.
Torrance, CA 90501
310-781-3808
Products: cosmetics, dental,
fragrance, hair care,
household, nail care, skin
care, sun care, toiletries,
bathing supply, soap,
shaving supply, vitamins
Availability: independent
sales representatives

Sunrise Lane
780 Greenwich St., Dept. PT
New York, NY 10014
212-242-7014
Products: baby care,
cosmetics, dental, hair care,
hair color, permanents,
household, bleach, laundry
detergent, hypo-allergenic
skin care, sun care, toiletries,
bathing, deodorant, soap,
shaving supply
Availability: mail order
MO

Sunshine Natural Products
Rte. 5P
Renick, WV 24966
304-497-3163
Products: companion animal
care, hair care, dandruff
shampoo
Availability: health food
stores, cooperatives
V MO

Sunshine Products Group
2545-A Prairie Rd.
Eugene, OR 97402
503-461-2160
800-285-6457
Products: essential oil,
herbal oil, body lotion,
massage oil, aromatherapy
Availability: health food
stores, drugstores, mail order
V MO

**Supreme Beauty Products
Company**
820 S. Michigan
Chicago, IL 60605
312-322-9444
800-272-6602
Products: hair care
Availability: drugstores
MO

Surrey, Inc.
13110 Trails End Rd.
Leander, TX 78641
512-267-7172
Products: toiletries, shaving
supply
Availability: health food
stores, drugstores, department stores, discount
department stores, supermarkets, distributors

Tammy Taylor Nails
18007E Skypark Cir.
Irvine, CA 92714
714-756-6606
800-748-6665
Products: cosmetics, skin care, hypo-allergenic skin care, nail care, sun care, toiletries
Availability: Tammy Taylor stores, mail order, distributors

TauT by Leonard Engelman
9428 Eton, #M
Chatsworth, CA 91311
818-773-3975
800-438-8288
Products: cosmetics, hypo-allergenic skin care for men and women, theatrical makeup
Availability: health food stores, beauty supply stores, mail order

Terra Nova
1200 Fifth St.
Berkeley, CA 94710
510-528-0666
Products: toiletries, fragrance, massage oil and lotion, skin care
Availability: department stores, health food stores, drugstores, boutiques, specialty stores, bath and fragrance stores

Terressentials
2650 Old National Pike
Middletown, MD 21769-8817
301-371-7333
Products: toiletries, hair care, baby care, companion animal care, household, books
Availability: mail order, Terressentials stores
V MO

Thursday Plantation Party Ltd.
330 E. Carrillo
Santa Barbara, CA 93101
805-963-2297
800-848-8966
Products: toiletries, dental hygiene, hair care, dandruff shampoo, hypo-allergenic skin care for men and women, sun care
Availability: health food stores, drugstores, supermarkets

Tisserand Aromatherapy, USA
P.O. Box 750428
Petaluma, CA 94975-0428
707-769-5120
Products: pure essential oil, hair care, massage oil and lotion, skin care for men and women, toiletries, aromatherapy
Availability: department stores, health food stores, boutiques, specialty stores, salons, spas, mail order
V MO

Tom's of Maine
P.O. Box 710
302 Lafayette Ctr.
Kennebunk, ME 04043
207-985-2944
800-367-8667
regisp@toms-of-maine.com
Products: baby care, dental hygiene, hair care, toiletries, deodorant, soap, shaving supply
Availability: drugstores, health food stores, supermarkets, cooperatives, Tom's of Maine stores, boutiques, specialty stores, mail order
MO

Tova Corporation
192 North Canon Dr.
Beverly Hills, CA 90210
310-246-0218
Products: skin care, hair care, fragrance
Availability: QVC, department stores, boutiques

Trader Joe's Company
P.O. Box 3270
538 Mission St.
South Pasadena, CA 91030
818-441-1177
Products: hair care, household, toiletries
Availability: Trader Joe's Company stores

Travel Mates America
1760 Lakeview Rd.
Cleveland, OH 44112
216-231-4102
Products: hair care, toiletries
Availability: private-label for hotel industry products only

Tressa, Inc.
P.O. Box 75320
Cincinnati, OH 45275
606-525-1300
800-879-8737
Products: hair care
Availability: professional beauty salons

TRI Hair Care Products
1850 Redondo Ave.
Long Beach, CA 90804
303-232-6149
800-458-8874
Products: hair care
Availability: salons, mail order

Trophy Animal Health Care
2796 Helen St.
Pensacola, FL 32504
904-476-7087
800-336-7087
Products: companion
animal care
Availability: select distributors, select companion
animal supply stores, mail
order

Tropical Botanicals, Inc.
P.O. Box 1354
15920 Via del Alba
Rancho Santa Fe, CA 92067
619-756-1265
800-777-1428
Products: hair care,
toiletries, sun care
Availability: health food
stores, cooperatives,
supermarkets, drugstores,
Nordstrom's in Southern
California, department
stores

Tropix Suncare Products
217 S. Seventh St., Suite 104
Brainerd, MN 56401
800-421-7314
Products: sun care
Availability: tanning salons
V

**Truly Moist (Desert
Naturels, Inc.)**
74-940 Hwy. 111, Suite 437
Indian Wells, CA 92201
619-346-1604
800-243-4435
Products: hypo-allergenic
skin care for men and
women
Availability: health food
stores, drugstores

**Tyra Skin Care for Men and
Women, Inc.**
9019 Oso Ave., Suite A
Chatsworth, CA 91311
818-407-1274
Products: hypo-allergenic
skin care for men and
women, sun care
Availability: department
stores, boutiques, specialty
stores, mail order
MO

Ultimate Life
P.O. Box 31154
Santa Barbara, CA 93130
805-962-2221
800-THE-MEAL
Products: instant meals
offering optimum nutrition
Availability: health food
stores, mail order, health
care practitioners, health
clubs
V MO

Ultima II (Revlon)
625 Madison Ave.
New York, NY 10022
212-572-5000
Products: cosmetics
Availability: department
stores

**Ultra Glow Cosmetics
(Nickull-Dowdall)**
P.O. Box 1469, Station A
Vancouver, B.C. V6C 2P7
Canada
604-939-3329
Products: cosmetics, sun
care, theatrical makeup
Availability: drugstores,
department stores, boutiques,
specialty stores, mail
order
V MO

**Upper Canada Soap &
Candle Makers**
1510 Caterpillar Rd.
Mississauga L4X 2W9
Canada
905-897-1710
Products: toiletries, soap,
candles
Availability: gift stores

Urban Decay
600 California St., Suite 1850
San Francisco, CA 94108
415-616-0415
dsoward@ix.netcom.com
Products: cosmetics, hair
color, nail care
Availability: department
stores

USA King's Crossing, Inc.
P.O. Box 832074
Richardson, TX 75083
214-680-9663
Products: all-natural shaving
oil for body care, razors,
razor blades, skin care for
men and women
Availability: health food
stores, mail order, specialty
stores, drugstores
V MO

**U.S. Sales Service (Crystal
Orchid)**
1414 E. Libra Dr.
Tempe, AZ 85283
602-839-3761
800-487-2633
Products: skin care, sun
care, toiletries, deodorant
stones, soap
Availability: health food
stores, cooperatives,
boutiques, specialty stores,
distributors, salons, mail order
V MO

Vapor Products
P.O. Box 568395
Orlando, FL 32856-8395
407-851-6230
800-621-2943
Products: mold and mildew prevention
Availability: discount department stores, supermarkets, home depot, mail order
MO

Vegelatum (Green Mountain)
P.O. Box 51867
Bowling Green, KY 42101
502-843-3178
Products: skin care, synthetic petroleum jelly
Availability: health food stores, drugstores, cooperatives, mail order
V MO

Vermont Soapworks
76 Box 4459
Middlebury, VT 05733
802-388-4302
natural@vtsoap.com
Products: soap, aromatherapy, baby care, household
Availability: health food stores, cooperatives, fine pharmacies, supermarkets, department stores, specialty stores, drugstores, mail order
MO

Veterinarian's Best, Inc.
P.O. Box 4459
Santa Barbara, CA 93103
805-963-5609
800-866-PETS
Products: companion animal care
Availability: companion animal supply stores, groomers, health food stores, companion animal catalogs, cooperatives, mail order
V MO

Victoria's Secret
4 Limited Pkwy.
Reynoldsburg, OH 43068
614-577-7111
Products: toiletries, fragrance and skin care for women, sun care
Availability: Victoria's Secret stores, mail order
MO

Virginia Soap, Ltd.
Group 60, Box 20, R.R. 1
Anola, Manitoba R0E 0A0
Canada
204-866-3788
Products: toiletries, aromatherapy
Availability: health food stores, drugstores, gift stores, mail order
MO

V'tae Parfum & Body Care
576 Searls Ave.
Nevada City, CA 95959
916-265-4255
800-643-3011
Products: aromatherapy, fragrance, household, air freshener, candles, massage oil and lotion, bathing supply, natural fragrance for body and environment
Availability: department stores, health food stores, cooperatives, V'tae Parfume & Body Care stores, boutiques, specialty stores, mail order
MO

Wachters' Organic Sea Products Corp.
360 Shaw Rd.
S. San Francisco, CA 94080
415-588-9567
800-682-7100
Products: companion animal care, hair care, household, laundry detergent, vitamins,
Availability: independent sales representatives, mail order, natural food stores
MO

Wala-Heilmittel
P.O. Box 407
Wyoming, RI 02898
401-539-7037
Products: skin care, toiletries
Availability: health food stores

Warm Earth Cosmetics
1155 Stanley Ave.
Chico, CA 95928-6944
916-895-0455
warm earth@ix.netcom.com
Products: cosmetics
Availability: health food stores, drugstores, supermarkets, mail order
V MO

Legend

- 🖾 Company uses Caring Consumer product logo
- V Vegan symbol (products contain no animal ingredients)
- MO Mail order available

WARM Store
31 Mill Hill Rd.
Woodstock, NY 12498
914-679-4242
Products: hair care, body
care, sun care, toiletries,
vitamins, companion animal
care
Availability: retail store in
Woodstock, N.Y.

Weleda, Inc.
P.O. Box 249
Congers, NY 10920
914-268-8572
800-289-1969
Products: aromatherapy,
baby care, dental, hair care,
skin care, toiletries, bathing
supply, deodorant, soap
Availability: drugstores,
health food stores, supermarkets, cooperatives, Weleda
stores, boutiques, specialty
stores, mail order
MO

Wella Corporation
524 Grand Ave.
Englewood, NJ 07631
201-930-1020
Products: hair care, hair
color, permanents, dandruff
shampoo, Gucci products
Availability: supermarkets,
drugstores, discount department stores, distributors

Wellington Laboratories, Inc.
2488 Townsgate Rd., Unit C
Wesstlake Village, CA 91361
805-495-2455
800-835-8118
Products: baby care, hypo-
allergenic skin care,
toiletries, shaving supply
Availability: distributors,
drugstores, supermarkets,
boutiques, specialty stores,
discount department stores,
department stores, cooperatives
MO

Whip-It Products, Inc.
P.O. Box 30128
Pensacola, FL 32503
904-436-2125
800-582-0398
Products: all-purpose
cleaning supply for home
and industrial use, oven
cleaning supply, carpet/rug
cleaning supply
Availability: distributors,
independent sales representatives, mail order
V MO

Wind River Herbs
P.O. Box 3876
Jackson, WY 83001
307-733-6731
Products: herbal medicine
Availability: health food
stores, clinics, mail order
MO

**Wisdom Toothbrush
Company**
151 S. Ptingstent Rd.
Deerfield, IL 60015
847-272-2040
800-628-4798
70702.1765@compuserve.com
Products: dental hygiene,
toothbrushes, dental floss
Availability: drugstores, mail
order, dentists
MO

WiseWays Herbals
Singing Brook Farm
99 Harvey Rd.
Worthington, MA 01098
413-238-4268
Products: aromatherapy,
baby care, companion
animal care, hair care, skin
care, toiletries, bathing
supply, shaving supply
Availability: drugstores,
health food stores, supermarkets, cooperatives, specialty
stores, mail order
MO

**Womankind (formerly New
Cycle Products)**
P.O. Box 1775
Sebastopol, CA 95472
707-522-8662
Products: cloth menstrual
pads, feminine hygiene
Availability: health food
stores, supermarkets,
boutiques, independent
sales representatives,
specialty stores, cooperatives, mail order
MO

Woods of Windsor USA, Ltd.
125 Mineola Ave., Suite 304
Roslyn Heights, NY 11577
516-625-1616
800-969-SCENT
Products: fragrance,
household, air freshener,
toiletries, bathing supply,
soap, shaving supply,
potpourri, sachets, scented
drawer liners
Availability: department
stores, drugstores, boutiques,
specialty stores, mail order
MO

Wysong Corporation
1880 N. Eastman Rd.
Midland, MI 48642-7779
517-631-0009
800-748-0188
wysong@tm.net
Products: hair care, sun care
vitamins, toiletries, shaving
supply
Availability: health food
stores
MO

Zia Cosmetics
410 Townsend St., 2nd Fl.
San Francisco, CA 94107-
1524
415-543-7546
800-334-7546
Products: naturally based
skin care for men and
women, cosmetics, sun care,
aromatherapy, body
moisturizer
Availability: health food
stores, cooperatives,
boutiques, specialty stores,
mail order
MO

68

256 pages, paperback
Item No. BK601 $10.00

FREE THE ANIMALS!
by Ingrid Newkirk

The voice that speaks for the animals speaks for the ALF (Animal Liberation Front). At long last, the story of the ALF in America is told, by PETA cofounder Ingrid Newkirk. Scintillating details about animals rescued from testing laboratories, fur farms, and food factories make for fast-moving adventure and riveting reading. Ingrid's interviews with the stop-at-nothing, dedicated ALF leader "Valerie" and her 10-year struggle to revolutionize society's attitudes toward animals provide a behind-the-scenes look at the ALF that surpasses everything you've ever heard in the media about this shadowy group.

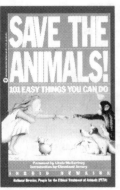

208 pages, paperback
Item No. BK590 $4.95

SAVE THE ANIMALS!
101 EASY THINGS YOU CAN DO
by Ingrid Newkirk

"Even the opposition must recognize an unusually fair and clear-minded spirit in Ms. Newkirk. If we all follow her reasonable, well-considered suggestions, we will soon rectify the horrible wrongs and see the end of cruelty to our fellow creatures."
Rue McClanahan

234 pages, paperback
Item No. BK205 $6.99

KIDS CAN SAVE THE ANIMALS! 101 EASY THINGS TO DO
by Ingrid Newkirk

All over the world, our animal friends are in trouble. That's the bad news. The good news is that kids can make a difference. Here is a book full of fascinating facts about animals, wonderful, whimsical drawings, and more than 100 projects and ideas that show how kids can help. Ages 8-13.

These books were created for those people who care enough about their fellow Earthlings to do something for them. It has never been so easy, or so important, to make a difference. Read, digest, share, and act!
Proceeds from the sale of these publications support PETA's programs in behalf of animals.
Ingrid E. Newkirk

To order, write PETA Merchandise, 501 Front St., Norfolk, VA 23510, or call 1-800-483-4366 (orders only, please) between 9:00 a.m. & 5:00 p.m. EST, Monday through Friday.

Quick Reference Guide

71

WHAT WOULD YOU DO TO SAVE AN ANIMAL?

Animals have long held a special place in my heart—their companionship has always been very important to me. That's why it distresses me to tell you that tens of thousands of animals are suffering needlessly,.

They desperately need help-and organizations like PETA.

Since 1980, People for the Ethical Treatment of Animals has become this nation's most effective advocate in behalf of animal protection. The people at PETA are committed to exposing and stopping animal cruelty—especially in laboratories.

It feels great to use my voice for animals. Please join me and contact PETA today. *You* can help save animals, too.

For more information on how you can become part of this vital work, write: PETA, 501 Front St., Norfolk, VA 23510, or call 757-622-PETA.

Rue

75

77

HYPO-ALLERGENIC SKIN CARE

GOOD **INTENTIONS** ARE **NOT** GOOD **ENOUGH**!

Be a Caring Consumer... Choose Cruelty-Free!

I DON'T CARE ABOUT THE POOR
I DON'T CARE ABOUT THE SICK
RE ABOUT THE HOMELESS
E ABOUT THE ANIMALS
RE ABOUT THEIR PAIN
OUT LOOKING CRASS
THE EARTH

I WEAR FUR BECAUSE
I DON'T CARE

If you **DO** care about something other than your own vanity, contact us and we'll show you how we can all share in a better world.

 PEOPLE FOR THE ETHICAL TREATMENT OF ANIMALS
501 FRONT ST., NORFOLK, VA 23510 ☎ 757-622-PETA

COMPANIES THAT TEST ON ANIMALS

Why Are These Companies Included on the "Do Test" List?

The following companies, pages 90-92, manufacture products that <u>ARE</u> tested on animals. Those marked with an asterisk (*) are presently observing a moratorium on animal testing. Please encourage them to announce a permanent ban. Listed in parentheses are either examples of products manufactured by that company or, if applicable, its parent company. Companies on this list may manufacture individual lines of products without animal testing (e.g., Del Laboratories claims its Naturistics and Natural Glow lines are not animal-tested). They have not, however, eliminated animal testing on their entire line of cosmetics and household products.

Similarly, companies on this list may make some products, such as pharmaceuticals, that are required by law to be tested on animals. However, the reason for these companies' inclusion is not the *required* animal testing that they conduct, but rather the animal testing of personal care and household products that is *not* required by law.

What Can Be Done About Animal Tests Required by Law?

Although animal testing of certain pharmaceuticals and chemicals is still mandated by law, the same arguments against using animals in cosmetics testing are valid when applied to the pharmaceutical and chemical industries. These industries are regulated by the Food and Drug Administration and the Environmental Protection Agency, respectively, and the laws that they enforce requiring animal tests were developed haphazardly in the 1920s. We know that non-animal test methods exist *right now* and that these tests are more accurate in predicting toxicity than are crude, cruel tests on animals. It is the responsibility of the companies that kill animals in order to bring their products to market to convince the regulatory agencies that there is a better way to determine product safety. Companies resist progress, because the crude nature of animal tests allows them to market many products that might be determined too toxic if cell culture tests were used. Let companies know how you feel about this.

Alberto-Culver (Tresemmé, TCB Naturals, Alberto VO5, Sally Beauty Supply)
2525 W. Armitage Ave.
Melrose Park, IL 60160
708-450-3000
www.alberto.com

Allergan, Inc.
2525 Dupont Dr.
P.O. Box 19534
Irvine, CA 92612
714-752-4500
800-347-4500
corpinfo@allergan.com

Arm & Hammer (Church & Dwight)
469 N. Harrison St.
Princeton, NJ 08543
609-683-5900
800-524-1328
www.armhammer.com

Aziza (Chesebrough-Ponds)
33 Benedict Place
Greenwich, CT 06830
203-661-2000
800-243-5804

Bausch & Lomb (Curél, Soft Sense, Clear Choice)
1 Bausch & Lomb Place
Rochester, NY 14604-2701
716-338-5386
800-344-8815
www.bausch.com

Benckiser (Coty, Lancaster, Jovan)
237 Park Ave., 19th Fl.
New York, NY 10017-3142
212-850-2300
attmail@cotyusa.com

Bic Corporation
500 Bic Dr.
Milford, CT 06460
203-783-2000

Block Drug Co., Inc. (Polident, Sensodyne, Tegrin, Lava, Carpet Fresh)
257 Cornelison Ave.
Jersey City, NJ 07302
201-434-3000
800-365-6500
blockdrug.com

Boyle-Midway (Reckitt & Colman)
2 Wickman Rd.
Toronto, Ontario
M8Z 5M5 Canada
416-255-2300

*Braun (Gillette Company)
400 Unicorn Clark Dr.
Woburn, MA 01801
800-272-8611
braun_usa@braun.de

Bristol-Myers Squibb Co. (Clairol, Ban Roll-On, Keri, Final Net)
345 Park Ave.
New York, NY 10154
212-546-4000
www.bms.com

Carter-Wallace (Arrid, Lady's Choice, Nair, Pearl Drops)
1345 Ave. of the Americas
New York, NY 10105
212-339-5000

Chesebrough-Ponds (Fabergé, Cutex, Vaseline)
800 Sylvan Ave.
Englewood Cliffs, NJ 07632
201-512-0094

Church & Dwight (Arm & Hammer)
469 N. Harrison St.
Princeton, NJ 08543
609-683-5900
800-524-1328

Clairol, Inc. (Bristol-Myers Squibb)
345 Park Ave.
New York, NY 10154
212-546-5000
800-223-5800
www.bms.com

Clorox (Pine-Sol, S.O.S., Tilex, ArmorAll)
P.O. Box 24305
Oakland, CA 94623-1305
510-271-7000
800-227-1860
info@clorox.com

Colgate-Palmolive Co. (Palmolive, Ajax, Fab, Speed Stick, Mennen, SoftSoap)
300 Park Ave.
New York, NY 10022
212-310-2000
800-221-4607
www.colgate.com

Coty (Benckiser)
237 Park Ave., 19th Fl.
New York, NY 10017-3142
212-850-2300
attmail@cotyusa.com

Dana Perfumes (Alyssa Ashley)
635 Madison Ave., 5th Fl.
New York, NY 10022-1009
212-751-3700
800-822-8547
www.beautyspot.com

Del Laboratories (Flame Glow, Commerce Drug, Sally Hansen)
565 Broad Hollow Rd.
Farmingdale, NY 11735
516-293-7070
800-645-9888
www.dellabs.com

*Dial Corporation (Purex, Renuzit)
1850 N. Central Ave.
Phoenix, AZ 85004
602-207-7100
800-528-0849

DowBrands (Glass Plus, Fantastik, Vivid)
P.O. Box 68511
Indianapolis, IN 46268
317-873-7000

Drackett Products Co. (S.C. Johnson & Son)
1525 Howe St.
Racine, WI 53403
414-631-2000
800-558-5252
www.scjohnsonwax.com

Ecolab, Inc.
370 N. Wabasha S.E.
St. Paul, MN 55102-1390
612-293-2233
800-352-5326

Erno Laszlo
200 First Stamford Place
3rd Fl.
Stamford, CT 06902-6759
203-363-5461

*Gillette Co. (Liquid Paper, Flair, Jafra, Braun, Oral B, Duracell)
Prudential Tower Bldg.
48th Fl.
Boston, MA 02199
617-421-7000
800-872-7202
braun_usa@braun.de

Givaudan-Roure
1775 Windsor Rd.
Teaneck, NJ 07666
201-833-2300

Helene Curtis Industries (Finesse, Unilever, Suave)
325 N. Wells St.
Chicago, IL 60610-4713
312-661-0222
www.unilever.com

Jhirmack (Playtex)
215 College Rd.
P.O. Box 728
Paramus, NJ 07653
201-295-8000
800-222-0453

Johnson & Johnson (Neutrogena)
1 Johnson & Johnson Plaza
New Brunswick, NJ 08933
908-524-0400
www.jnj.com

S.C. Johnson & Son (Pledge, Drano, Windex, Glade)
1525 Howe St.
Racine, WI 53403
414-631-2000
800-558-5252
www.scjohnsonwax.com

Kimberly-Clark Corp. (Kleenex, Scott Paper, Huggies)
P.O. Box 619100
Dallas, TX 75261-9100
800-544-1847
www.kimberly-clark.com

Lamaur
5601 E. River Rd.
Fridley, MN 55432
612-571-1234

L&F Products
One Philips Pkwy.
Montvale, NJ 07645-1810
201-573-5700

Lever Bros. (Unilever)
390 Park Ave.
New York, NY 10022
212-888-1260
800-745-9696
www.unilever.com

*Mary Kay Cosmetics
16251 N. Dallas Pkwy.
Dallas, TX 75248
214-687-6300
800-201-1362
www.marykay.com

Mead
Courthouse Plaza N.E.
Dayton, OH 45463
513-222-6323
www.mead.com

Mennen Co. (Colgate-Palmolive)
E. Hanover Ave.
Morristown, NJ 07962
201-631-9000
www.colgate.com

Murphy-Phoenix Co. (Colgate-Palmolive)
P.O. Box 39670
Solon, OH 44139
800-486-7627
www.colgate.com

Neoteric Cosmetics
4880 Havana St.
Denver, CO 80239-0019
303-373-4860

Neutron Industries, Inc.
7107 N. Black Canyon Hwy.
Phoenix, AZ 85021
602-864-0090

Noxell (Procter & Gamble)
11050 York Rd.
Hunt Valley, MD 21030-2098
410-785-7300
800-572-3232
www.pg.com

Olay Co./Oil of Olay (Procter & Gamble)
P.O. Box 599
Cincinnati, OH 45201
800-543-1745
www.pg.com

*Oral-B (Gillette Company)
1 Lagoon Dr.
Redwood City, CA 94065-1561
415-598-5000
www.oralb.com

Pantene (Procter & Gamble)
Procter & Gamble Plaza
Cincinnati, OH 45202
800-945-7768
www.pg.com

Parfums International
(White Shoulders)
1345 Ave. of the Americas
New York, NY 10105
212-261-1000

*Parker Pens (Gillette
Company)
P.O. Box 5100
Janesville, WI 53547-5100
608-755-7000
braun_usa@braun.de

Perrigo
117 Water St.
Allegan, MI 49010
616-673-8451
800-253-3606
www.perrigo.com

Pfizer, Inc. (Bain de Soleil,
Plax, Visine, Desitin,
BenGay)
235 E. 42nd St.
New York, NY 10017
212-573-2323
www.pfizer.com

Physicians Formula
Cosmetics (Pierre Fabré)
1055 W. Eighth St.
Azusa, CA 91702
818-334-3395

Playtex Products, Inc.
(Banana Boat, Woolite)
215 College Rd.
Paramus, NJ 07653
201-265-8000

Procter & Gamble Co.
(Crest, Tide, Cover Girl,
Max Factor, Giorgio)
P.O. Box 599
Cincinnati, OH 45201
513-983-1100
800-543-1745
www.pg.com

Reckitt & Colman (Lysol,
Mop & Glo)
1655 Valley Rd.
Wayne, NJ 07474-0945
201-633-6700
800-232-9665

Richardson-Vicks (Procter &
Gamble)
P.O. Box 599
Cincinnati, OH 45201
513-983-1100
800-543-1745
www.pg.com

Sally Hansen (Del Laboratories)
565 Broad Hollow Rd.
Farmingdale, NY 11735
516-293-7070
800-645-9888
www.dellabs.com

Sanofi (Yves Saint Laurent)
90 Park Ave., 24th Fl.
New York, NY 10016
212-907-2000

Schering-Plough
(Coppertone)
2000 Galloping Hill Rd.
Kenilworth, NJ 07033
908-298-4000
800-842-4090
www.myhealth.com

Schick (Warner-Lambert)
201 Tabor Rd.
Morris Plains, NJ 07950
201-540-2000
800-492-1555
www.warner-lambert.com

SmithKline Beecham
100 Beecham Dr.
Pittsburgh, PA 15205
412-928-1000
800-456-6670
www.sb.com

Softsoap Enterprises
(Colgate-Palmolive)
1107 Hazeltine Blvd., Suite
370
Chaska, MN 55318
612-448-1118
www.colgate.com

Sunshine Makers (Simple
Green)
P.O. Box 2708
Huntington Beach, CA
92649
714-840-1319
800-228-0709
www.simplegreen.com

Sun Star
600 Eagle Dr.
Bensenville, IL 60106-1977
800-821-5455

3M (Scotch, Post-It)
Center Bldg., 220-2E-02
St. Paul, MN 55144-1000
612-733-1110
800-364-3577
www.3m.com

Unilever (Lever Bros.,
Calvin Klein, Elizabeth
Arden, Helene Curtis)
390 Park Ave.
New York, NY 10022
212-888-1260
800-745-9696
www.unilever.com

Vidal Sassoon (Procter &
Gamble)
P.O. Box 599
Cincinnati, OH 45201
800-543-1745
www.pg.com

Warner-Lambert
(Lubriderm, Listerine,
Schick)
201 Tabor Rd.
Morris Plains, NJ 07950
201-540-2000
800-323-5379
www.warner-lambert.com

Westwood Pharmaceuticals
100 Forest Ave.
Buffalo, NY 14213
716-887-3400
800-333-0950

ALTERNATIVES TO LEATHER
AND
OTHER ANIMAL PRODUCTS

Many animals from whom skins and other body parts are obtained suffer all the horrors of factory farming, including extreme crowding and confinement, deprivation, unanesthetized castration, branding, tail-docking and de-horning, and cruel treatment during transport and slaughter. As a result, more and more people are realizing that animal products are something we can do without.

Alternatives to leather can be found just about anywhere you might shop. But some places, such as discount shoe and variety stores, like Payless Shoe Source, Fayva, Kmart, J.C. Penney, Marshall's, and Wal-Mart, offer larger selections. Designers like Liz Claiborne, Capezio, Sam & Libby, Unlisted by Kenneth Cole, and Nike (call 1-800-344-NIKE for a current list of vegan styles) offer an array of nonleather handbags, wallets, and shoes.

For more shopping tips, send for *The Compassionate Shopper* (Beauty Without Cruelty, 175 W. 12th St., #16G, New York, NY 10011-8275) or "A Shopper's Guide to Leather Alternatives" (The Vegetarian Resource Group, P.O. Box 1463, Baltimore, MD 21203).

The following is a list of mail-order companies that specialize in nonleather clothing and accessories:

Aesop, Inc.
P.O. Box 315
N. Cambridge, MA 02140
617-628-8030

Creatureless Comforts
702 Page St.
Stoughton, MA 02072
617-344-7496

ExTredz
7015 Ordan Dr.
Unit 12-14
Mississauga, Ontario
L5T 1Y2 Canada
800-665-9182

Heartland Products
Box 218
Dakota City, IA 50529
800-441-4692

The Ohio Hempery
7002 State Rte. 329
Guysville, OH 45735
800-BUY-HEMP

Pangea
7829 Woodmont Ave.
Bethesda, MD 20814
301-652-3181

Used Rubber USA
597 Haight St.
San Francisco, CA 94117
415-626-7855

Vegetarian Shoes
12 Gardner St.
Brighton BN1 1UP
England
011-441-273-691913

CUT OUT CRUELTY!

As a service to caring consumers,
these cruelty-free companies
offer you discount coupons or free samples.

Using these coupons makes it easier than
ever to be a compassionate shopper.

*Now you can save cash
while you save animals!*

**PETA'S
1998
Shopping
Guide for
Caring
Consumers**
Redeemable
through
company only.

**PETA'S
1998
Shopping
Guide for
Caring
Consumers**
Redeemable
through
company only.

**PETA'S
1998
Shopping
Guide for
Caring
Consumers**
Redeemable
through
company only.

**PETA'S
1998
Shopping
Guide for
Caring
Consumers**
Redeemable
through
company only.

**PETA'S
1998
Shopping
Guide for
Caring
Consumers**
Redeemable
through
company only.

**PETA'S
1998
Shopping
Guide for
Caring
Consumers**
Redeemable
through
company only.

**PETA'S
1998
Shopping
Guide for
Caring
Consumers**
Redeemable
through
company only.

**PETA'S
1998
Shopping
Guide for
Caring
Consumers**
Redeemable
through
company only.

PETA'S 1998 Shopping Guide for Caring Consumers
Redeemable through company only.

PETA'S 1998 Shopping Guide for Caring Consumers
Redeemable through company only.

PETA'S 1998 Shopping Guide for Caring Consumers
Redeemable through company only.

PETA'S 1998 Shopping Guide for Caring Consumers
Redeemable through company only.

PETA'S 1998 Shopping Guide for Caring Consumers
Redeemable through company only.

PETA'S 1998 Shopping Guide for Caring Consumers
Redeemable through company only.

PETA'S 1998 Shopping Guide for Caring Consumers
Redeemable through company only.

PETA'S 1998 Shopping Guide for Caring Consumers
Redeemable through company only.

**PETA'S
1998
Shopping
Guide for
Caring
Consumers**
Redeemable
through
company only.

**PETA'S
1998
Shopping
Guide for
Caring
Consumers**
Redeemable
through
company only.

**PETA'S
1998
Shopping
Guide for
Caring
Consumers**
Redeemable
through
company only.

**PETA'S
1998
Shopping
Guide for
Caring
Consumers**
Redeemable
through
company only.

**PETA'S
1998
Shopping
Guide for
Caring
Consumers**
Redeemable
through
company only.

**PETA'S
1998
Shopping
Guide for
Caring
Consumers**
Redeemable
through
company only.

**PETA'S
1998
Shopping
Guide for
Caring
Consumers**
Redeemable
through
company only.

**PETA'S
1998
Shopping
Guide for
Caring
Consumers**
Redeemable
through
company only.

PETA'S 1998 Shopping Guide for Caring Consumers
Redeemable through company only.

PETA'S 1998 Shopping Guide for Caring Consumers
Redeemable through company only.

PETA'S 1998 Shopping Guide for Caring Consumers
Redeemable through company only.

PETA'S 1998 Shopping Guide for Caring Consumers
Redeemable through company only.

PETA'S 1998 Shopping Guide for Caring Consumers
Redeemable through company only.

PETA'S 1998 Shopping Guide for Caring Consumers
Redeemable through company only.

PETA'S 1998 Shopping Guide for Caring Consumers
Redeemable through company only.

PETA'S 1998 Shopping Guide for Caring Consumers
Redeemable through company only.

What Is PETA?

People for the Ethical Treatment of Animals (PETA) is an international nonprofit organization dedicated to exposing and eliminating all animal abuse. PETA uses public education, litigation, research and investigations, media campaigns, and involvement at the grassroots level to accomplish this goal.

With the help of our dedicated members, PETA persuades major corporations to stop testing products on animals; advocates alternatives to eating animals by promoting a vegetarian diet; and has forced the closure of federally funded animal research facilities because of animal abuses.

To help stop the exploitation and abuse of animals, become a PETA member today.

MEMBERSHIP & DONATION FORM

Enclosed is my contribution to go toward your vital work on behalf of all animals.

❏ $15 ❏ $25 ❏ $50 ❏ $100 ❏ Other $_____

(Annual membership is $15.00. Members receive PETA's *Guide to Compassionate Living* and a subscription to PETA's quarterly newsletter.)

❏ I'm already a PETA member. This is an extra donation.

Name _____

Address _____

City _____ State _____ Zip _____

Complete this form and send with your check to:

PeTA 501 Front Street, Norfolk, VA 23510

Thank you from all of us at PETA. .